SYSTEMATIC GUIDE TO PERSPECTIVE
A Step-by-Step Handbook
for the Classroom and the Professional

by Rocco Leonardis, Architect RA-RIBA-NCARB

New York School of Interior Design
New York, NY

"Arrangement includes the putting of things in their proper places and the elegance of effect which is due to adjustments appropriate to the character of the work. Its forms of expression are these: groundplan, elevation, and perspective."

--from Chapter II, The Fundamental Principles of Architecture,
THE TEN BOOKS OF ARCHITECTURE
by Marcus Vitruvius, translated by Morris Hicky Morgan

Library of Congress Catalog Card Number: 97-75490
ISBN: 1-890053-01-5

Copyright © 1998 by Rocco Leonardis

Printed in the United States of America.

All drawings and text by Rocco Leonardis.

With many thanks to Dorothy Irwin for her editing, rewriting, and inspiration.

Photo credits: All photographs by Rocco Leonardis. Pgs. 14, 15: With permission of the Morris-Jumel Mansion Museum.

Published by the New York School of Interior Design
170 East 70th Street, New York, NY 10021-5110

TABLE OF CONTENTS

PREFACE

This book explains and demonstrates step-by-step how to construct accurate one-point and two-point perspective drawings. The book is complete in itself, and differs from other similar works in that it clearly demonstrates the principles on which the practical rules of perspective are based. No other book like it exists.

Perspective is taught in thousands of classes, in many disciplines, throughout this country and around the world. Measured perspective is essential for the correct visualization of architectural designs, both exterior and interior, as well as stage sets, sculptures, paintings, murals, and more. This volume is especially designed for interior designers, architects, and scenic designers. It will also be very useful to sculptors and painters who are creating large works for either individual or public commissions.

The difficulty in learning perspective drawing as a measured system of visualization (a discipline which is hundreds of years old) is that although numerous works on the subject have been printed, few are of any practical use to those who actually want to "make real things." The authors either do too little or too much. In many cases, the author assumes an understanding by the reader at different steps in the process which the reader does not possess. Alternatively, an author may labor over each and every concept and construction to a point where the reader is simply overwhelmed. I know that the reader, whether a student or a professional, wants to get work done. The reader needs to use this book as a guide which will explain practically, logically, and, whenever possible, graphically the *how* and *why* of the process.

As a professional architect for over 35 years, I have taught perspective drawing without interruption for more than a decade. Students repeatedly ask the same questions about the subject. This book clarifies the most frequently encountered misconceptions and answers all questions. It is a no-nonsense, easy-to-read handbook which guides the reader through the correct construction of one-point and two-point perspective drawings.

INTRODUCTION

Many people think that perspective drawing is drafting. It is not; it is a science.

We perceive objects as getting smaller in size as their distance from us increases. Yet they actually remain the same size. All parallel lines appear to vanish to the same point on the horizon; streets with parallel sides, railroad tracks, and corridor walls appear to converge, even though we know they remain parallel. Because of our visual perceptions, all human beings exist in a realm of illusion rather than in a measured reality.

Not unlike Plato's Myth of the Cave, perceived reality is an approximation of the measured truth. In determining measured depth of field, perspective drawing combines the phenomenon of sight (the reduction in size of objects in relation to their distance from the observer, and the convergence of parallel lines) with a very simple concept from plane geometry. The geometric concept is this: All parallel lines, when crossed by a line, produce angles which are both equal and opposite of each other. That is, when a series of parallel lines is crossed by a line at 45 degrees, the resulting equal measurements produce a net of squares. The inventor of Renaissance perspective, Brunelleschi, had thereby created a physical relationship between measured reality (plans and elevations) and the illusions of visual perception (depth of field). Although there is a great deal more to this procedure, experience in the classroom has shown that given a simple, true, strong base as theory, both the student and the teacher can build well.

The accurate drawing of objects in perspective is accomplished by the simple combination of two well-established principles:

1. For planes parallel to the ground floor plane, ALL PARALLEL LINES APPEAR TO VANISH AT THE SAME POINT ON THE HORIZON LINE.

2. Any line drawn through a series of equidistant parallel lines will produce equal and opposite angles (for the measuring point method).

The simple process for drawing objects in perspective is to reduce their shapes to a series of points, which have a pre-determined relationship to each other. This is achieved by covering with a grid, or throwing a net over, the subjects to be drawn and their related space. The grid, or net, is a series of straight, parallel, equidistant lines at 90 degrees to each other and at a scale.

All objects and subjects to be drawn are composed of a series of continuous points. Any point will have a relationship to the grid and therefore can be located in space. This concept allows for the location of planes not on the grid and therefore further potential point locations.

A POINT DOES NOT HAVE ANY SIZE OR DIMENSION. A POINT IS THOUGHT OF AS THE LOCATION WHERE TWO PLANES INTERSECT.

Before you begin a perspective drawing, accurate and drawn-to-scale PLANS and ELEVATIONS of the subjects to be drawn are essential. YOU MUST KNOW WHAT YOU ARE GOING TO DRAW BEFORE YOU CAN DRAW IT. You must know where the subjects to be drawn are in relationship to each other and to the space around them.

Students frequently ask what the difference is in making a choice between a one-point of a two-point perspective. It is the overall aspect of the view and the dominance of either one-point or two-point material within the general aspect that should determine the choice. As an example, you may have a room in which all of the furniture is parallel to the walls of the room. Because all parallel lines vanish at the same point, the choice between using a one-point or a two-point perspective should be based on what you wish to 'showcase' within your design. A one-point perspective is, in my opinion, the most profitable for an interior designer to draw: You get three walls as opposed to the two of a two-point, and you also will have more foreground than in a two-point. You are able to come in closer on your subject with your SP and have more usable floor and tabletop surface. You may then wish to draw a two-point aspect of the overall space, with every object within the space not being parallel to the two-point vanishing points, because you simply like the way it looks.

You are in control of the world that you create on paper.

There are two practical methods used to achieve perspective: Plan Projection and the Measuring Point. Both are included in this book. How should you decide which method to use? When using the Plan Projection method, you must work with the plan and the perspective on the same surface; they must also both be drawn at the same scale. On the other hand, the Measuring Point method allows you to have the plan and the perspective on separate surfaces and at different scales. Therefore, there is greater artistic freedom in using the Measuring Point method, because the perspective can take up a larger area and can be created without the distraction of an additional image. In addition to these advantages, the Measuring Point method is particularly suited to highly complex plans, since the points can be simply plotted on the grid, whereas the Plan Projection method requires a dense network of projected lines that must connect the plan to the perspective.

When using the Measuring Point, you can *see* the floor plane as a grid, and you can see where on it you wish to position various elements. By counting the squares, dividing the squares, or drawing 45 degree triangles in perspective to get depth of field, you are constantly aware of the plane on which you are working. In contrast, Plan Projection requires additional visualization to reinforce a mental image of the perspective. For every point you wish to locate in perspective, you must first establish a plane upon which it is to sit. The floor plane is implied and cannot be referenced in and of itself.

LIST OF ABBREVIATIONS

PP	=	Picture Plane
HL	=	Horizon Line
GL	=	Ground Line
CVR	=	Central Visual Ray
SP	=	Standing Point or Station Point
VP	=	Vanishing Point
VPR	=	Vanishing Point Right
VPL	=	Vanishing Point Left
MP	=	Measuring Point
MPR	=	Measuring Point Right
MPL	=	Measuring Point Left
DVP	=	Diagonal Vanishing Point: the 45 degree VP, coincidental with the MP in one-point perspective

DEFINITIONS

The Observer
This term refers to the person who is standing or sitting at the station point (SP). It is from the observer's point of view that the objects and space will be depicted.

SP = Standing Point or Station Point
The SP indicates the position of the observer, where the observer is standing or sitting or reclining.

HL = Horizon Line = eye level
Because the earth is curved, the surface of the globe will appear to pass through the level of the eyes of the observer, regardless of the height of the observer. Whether seated or standing, the observer sees the earth as a straight tangent line to the curve of the earth. The eye level of the observer of the drawing will be the HL of the drawing.

PP = Picture Plane
The PP is an infinite surface without thickness, both parallel and perpendicular to the observer. It is moveable and is the only place in perspective that you can measure with your scale (ruler). The PP is your reference plane. Keep the PP perpendicular to the observer's line of vision.

GL = Ground Line
The GL indicates the ground or floor plane. It is a reference plane; it is not necessarily the ground or the floor.

Whether the observer is sitting or standing at the beach, the water surface = HL will pass through the observer's eyes.

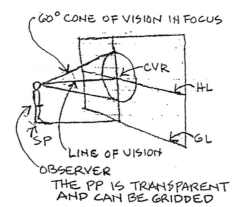

DEFINITIONS

CVR = Central Visual Ray
The CVR indicates the place on the HL (and also on the PP) where the observer is looking. The term is derived from the line of sight parallel to the ground plane and perpendicular to the PP. This line of sight is the axis of the cone of vision of the observer.

VP = Vanishing Point
All parallel lines that are parallel to the ground plane, appear to vanish at the same point on the HL. There will be as many VP's in the same drawing as there are different positions of objects and different positions of planes.

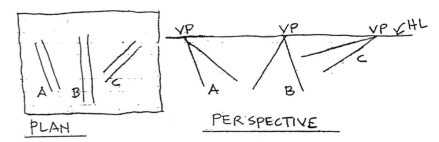

Cone of Vision
60 degrees revolves about the line of vision, originating from the third eye of the observer, in the direction of the PP and the object or space being observed. The axis of the cone of vision extends from the eye of the observer to the CVR on the HL. The area within that cone of vision is the area that is viewed by the observer as being in focus; the area outside of this cone of vision is out of focus to the observer. The cone of vision needs to be determined both in plan and elevation before the drawing is constructed because they will usually delineate different areas of focus. The cone of vision is what therefore determines the position or location of the observer = it locates the SP.

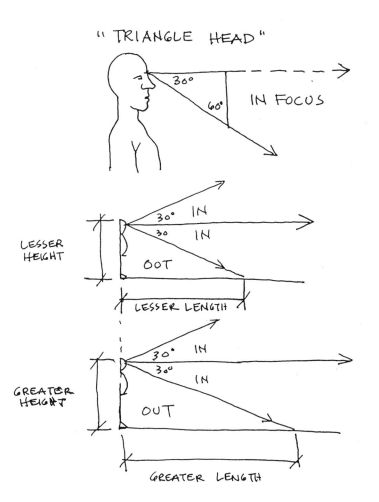

" TRIANGLE HEAD "

30°

60°   IN FOCUS

LESSER HEIGHT

30° IN
30   IN
OUT

LESSER LENGTH

GREATER HEIGHT

30° IN
30° IN
OUT

GREATER LENGTH

The Cone of Vision: In-Focus and Out-of-Focus

As if you were a cyclops and had only one eye in the middle of your forehead, place a 30 degree/60degree triangle between your eyes to demonstrate the principle of the cone of vision.

Using the 60 degree cone of vision, check the location of the observer (the SP) in both the plan and the elevation.

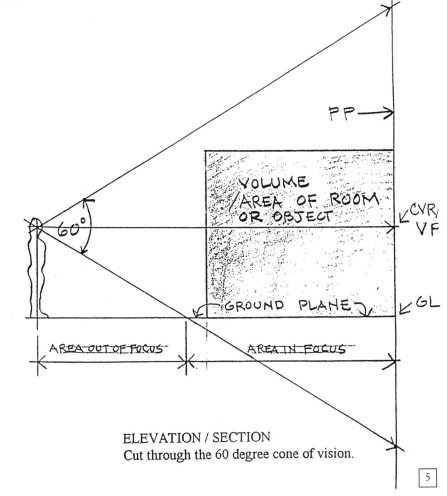

PP →

VOLUME / AREA OF ROOM OR OBJECT

60°

CVR / VF

GROUND PLANE

GL

AREA OUT OF FOCUS   AREA IN FOCUS

ELEVATION / SECTION
Cut through the 60 degree cone of vision.

When the SP is a different height in the same position, THE AMOUNT OF GROUND PLANE IN FOCUS IS DIFFERENT. You should always check the cone of vision in both the plan and the elevation; they are usually different. Use the one that best clarifies your design.

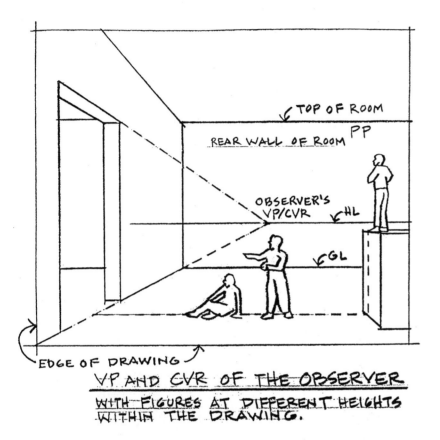

TOP OF ROOM

REAR WALL OF ROOM PP

OBSERVER'S
VP/CVR HL

GL

EDGE OF DRAWING

VP AND CVR OF THE OBSERVER
WITH FIGURES AT DIFFERENT HEIGHTS WITHIN THE DRAWING.

Each individual within the drawing may have a different eye height or horizon line. This is because when standing or sitting individuals have different heights above the ground or floor plane. However, the eye height of the observer of the whole composition is the eye height used for the drawing of the perspective. Likewise, the point on the horizon line that the observer is looking at { the CVR} is the controlling point used in constructing the perspective.

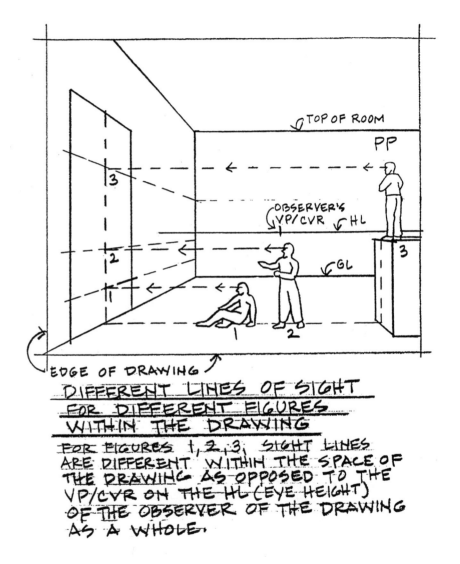

TOP OF ROOM

PP

3

OBSERVER'S
VP/CVR HL

2

GL

3

1   2

EDGE OF DRAWING

DIFFERENT LINES OF SIGHT
FOR DIFFERENT FIGURES
WITHIN THE DRAWING

FOR FIGURES 1, 2, 3, SIGHT LINES ARE DIFFERENT WITHIN THE SPACE OF THE DRAWING AS OPPOSED TO THE VP/CVR ON THE HL (EYE HEIGHT) OF THE OBSERVER OF THE DRAWING AS A WHOLE.

The difference between eye heights CVR's of figures within the drawing and the CVR of the whole drawing.

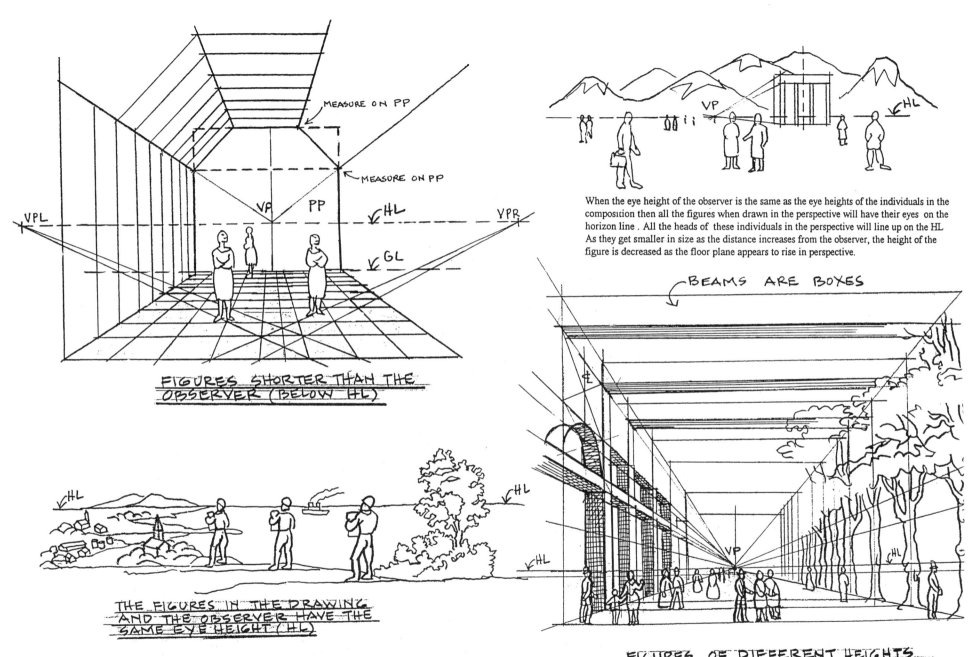

MEASURE ON PP

MEASURE ON PP

VP   PP

VPL   HL   VPR

GL

FIGURES SHORTER THAN THE OBSERVER (BELOW HL)

When the eye height of the observer is the same as the eye heights of the individuals in the composition then all the figures when drawn in the perspective will have their eyes on the horizon line . All the heads of these individuals in the perspective will line up on the HL As they get smaller in size as the distance increases from the observer, the height of the figure is decreased as the floor plane appears to rise in perspective.

VP   HL

HL   HL

THE FIGURES IN THE DRAWING AND THE OBSERVER HAVE THE SAME EYE HEIGHT (HL)

BEAMS ARE BOXES

VP   HL

FIGURES OF DIFFERENT HEIGHTS VANISH LIKE TELEPHONE POLES, TREES, OR COLUMNS TO THE V.P.

7

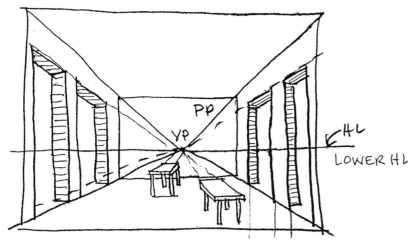

PP

VP

HL

LOWER HL

While standing in the same place and lowering the eye height of the observer (decreasing the distance between the GL and the HL), the less of the surface of the table tops and floor will be seen.

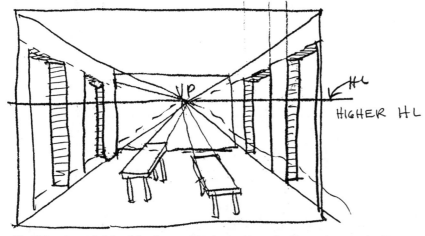

VP

HL

HIGHER HL

The higher the eye height of the observer (that is, the greater the distance between the GL and the HL), the more surface of the table tops and floor will be seen. As long as the table tops and floor are within the cone of vision.

HORIZON LINE RELATIONSHIPS

VIEWER ABOVE AND BELOW HL

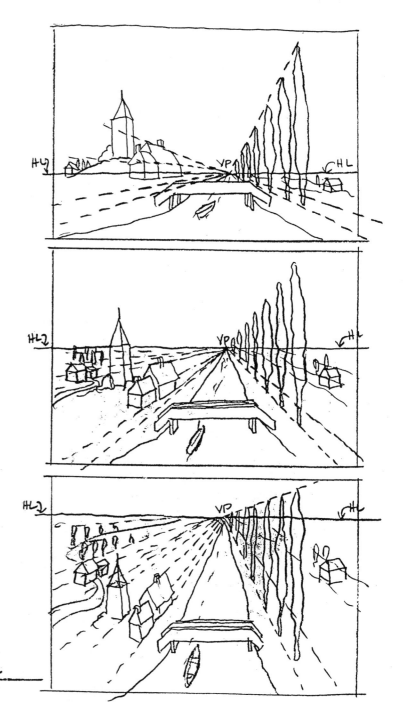

HL

VP

HL

HL

VP

HL

HL

VP

HL

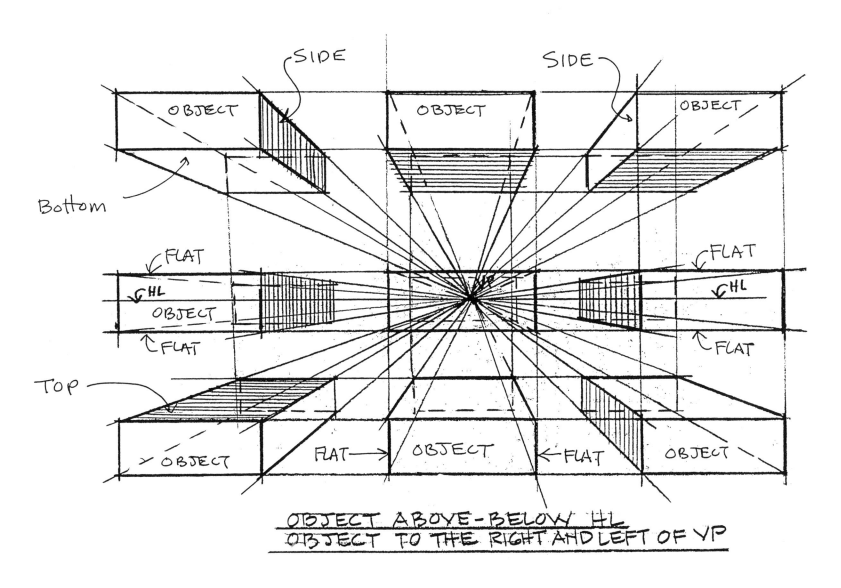

SIDE

SIDE

OBJECT

OBJECT

OBJECT

Bottom

FLAT

FLAT

HL

HL

OBJECT

FLAT

FLAT

TOP

OBJECT

FLAT →

OBJECT

← FLAT

OBJECT

OBJECT ABOVE - BELOW HL
OBJECT TO THE RIGHT AND LEFT OF VP

As the object or room to be viewed approaches the HL, it begins to lose its three-dimensional quality. This is because the surfaces making the corners with the horizontals are seen less as the horizontals begin to line up with the HL and thereby lose depth of field. The same loss of three-dimensionality occurs when the verticals of the object or space to be viewed begin to line up with the vertical center line that crosses the HL at the VP at 90 degrees.

PHOTO CAPTIONS

Figure 1: Sketch plan shows a pattern within a square. The pattern can be constructed from its diagonals and center lines.

Figure 2: The square, with the same diagonals and center lines, is now seen in perspective.

Figure 3: All parallel lines appear to vanish at the same point on the horizon line.

Figure 4 and 5: In long vistas, whether within an architectural context or not, the ground line and the horizon line appear close together.

Figure 6: In a one-point interior perspective, the walls of the room are parallel and perpendicular to the observer's line of sight.

Figure 7: In a two-point interior perspective, the walls may be at any angle to the observer's line of sight.

Figure 1

Figure 2

Figure 3

HL

GL

VP

Figure 4

HL
GL
VP

Figure 5

Figure 6

Figure 7

PLAN PROJECTION METHOD
One-Point Perspective and Two-Point Perspective

PLAN

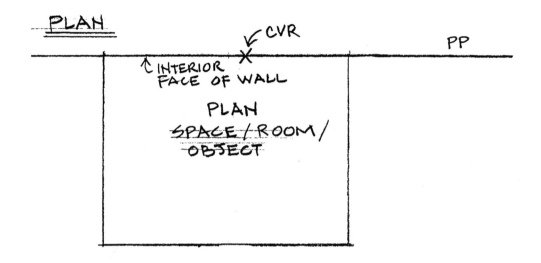

↙ CVR

PP

↖ INTERIOR
FACE OF WALL

PLAN
~~SPACE/ROOM/
OBJECT~~

STEP 1

FOR INTERIORS

Ⓐ PLACE PP AT BACK OF SPACE IN
LINE WITH INTERIOR FACE OF WALL

Ⓑ LOCATE CVR (WHERE - THE POINT - YOU
ARE LOOKING)

NOTE YOU CAN LOCATE THE CVR ANYWHERE
ON THE HL ON THE PP.

PLAN

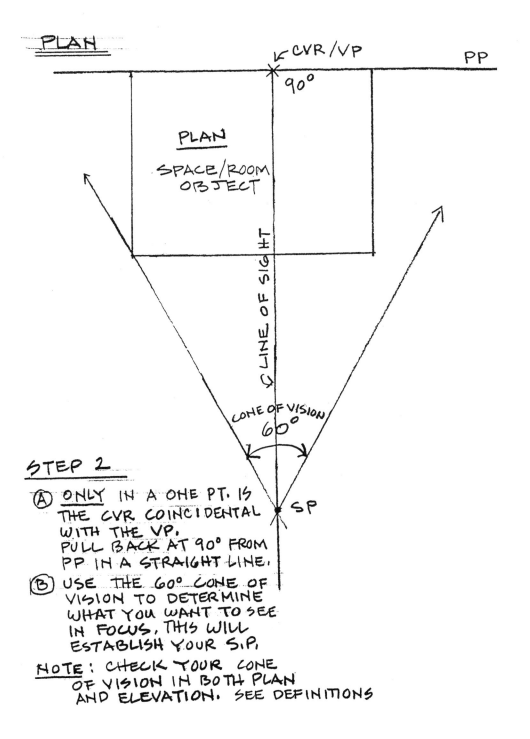

PP

← CVR/VP

90°

PLAN

SPACE/ROOM
OBJECT

LINE OF SIGHT

CONE OF VISION
60°

SP

STEP 2

(A) <u>ONLY</u> IN A ONE PT. IS
THE CVR COINCIDENTAL
WITH THE VP.
PULL BACK AT 90° FROM
PP IN A STRAIGHT LINE.

(B) USE THE 60° CONE OF
VISION TO DETERMINE
WHAT YOU WANT TO SEE
IN FOCUS. THIS WILL
ESTABLISH YOUR S.P.

<u>NOTE</u>: CHECK YOUR CONE
OF VISION IN BOTH PLAN
AND ELEVATION. SEE DEFINITIONS

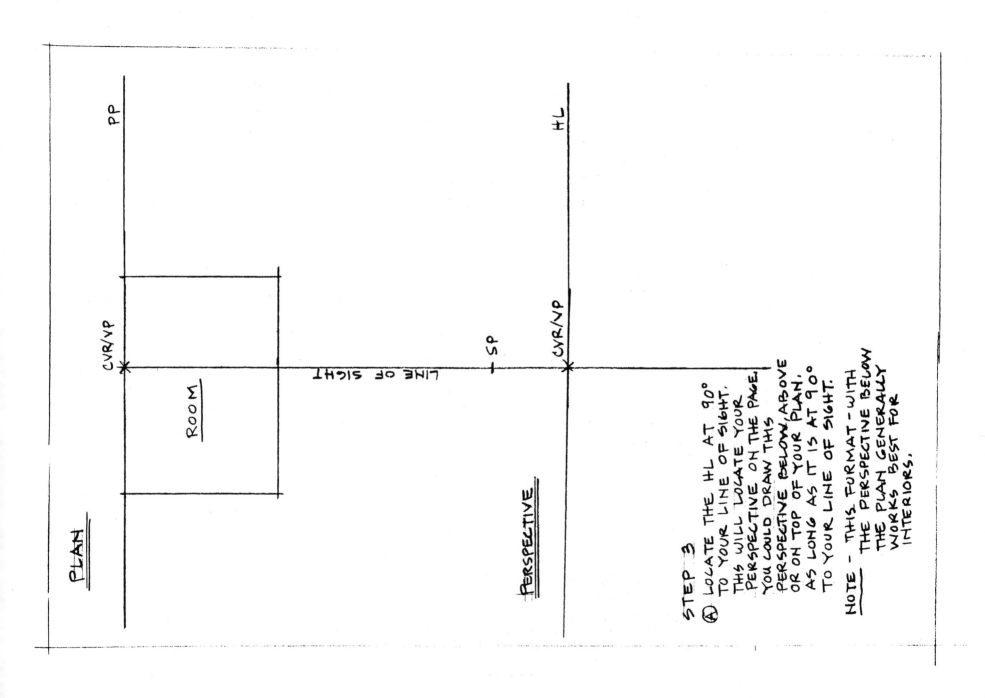

PLAN

PP

CVR/VP

ROOM

LINE OF SIGHT

SP

PERSPECTIVE

CVR/VP

HL

STEP 3

Ⓐ LOCATE THE HL AT 90°
TO YOUR LINE OF SIGHT.
THIS WILL LOCATE YOUR
PERSPECTIVE ON THE PAGE.
YOU COULD DRAW THIS
PERSPECTIVE BELOW/ABOVE
OR ON TOP OF YOUR PLAN,
AS LONG AS IT IS AT 90°
TO YOUR LINE OF SIGHT.

NOTE - THIS FORMAT - WITH
THE PERSPECTIVE BELOW
THE PLAN GENERALLY
WORKS BEST FOR
INTERIORS.

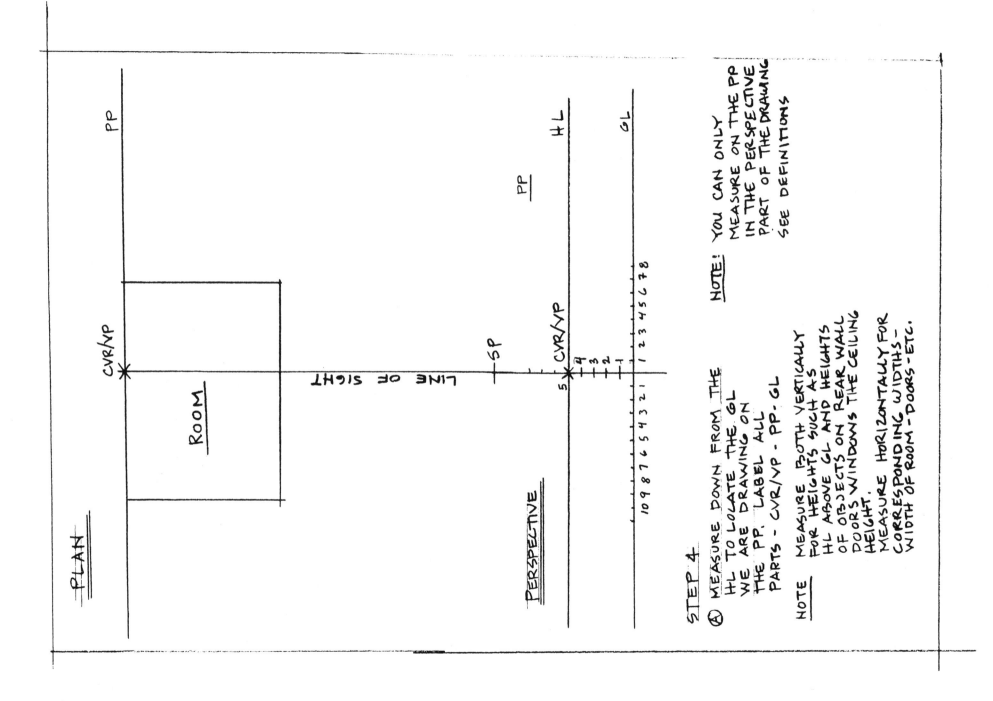

PLAN

PP

CVR/VP

ROOM

PERSPECTIVE

LINE OF SIGHT

SP

PP

HL

CVR/VP

4
3
2
1

10 9 8 7 6 5 4 3 2 1 1 2 3 4 5 6 7 8

GL

STEP 4

(A) MEASURE DOWN FROM THE
HL TO LOCATE THE GL
WE ARE DRAWING ON
THE PP. LABEL ALL
PARTS - CVR/VP - PP - GL

NOTE MEASURE BOTH VERTICALLY
FOR HEIGHTS SUCH AS
HL ABOVE GL AND HEIGHTS
OF OBJECTS ON REAR WALL
DOORS WINDOWS THE CEILING
HEIGHT.
MEASURE HORIZONTALLY FOR
CORRESPONDING WIDTHS -
WIDTH OF ROOM - DOORS - ETC.

NOTE! YOU CAN ONLY
MEASURE ON THE PP
IN THE PERSPECTIVE
PART OF THE DRAWING
SEE DEFINITIONS

21

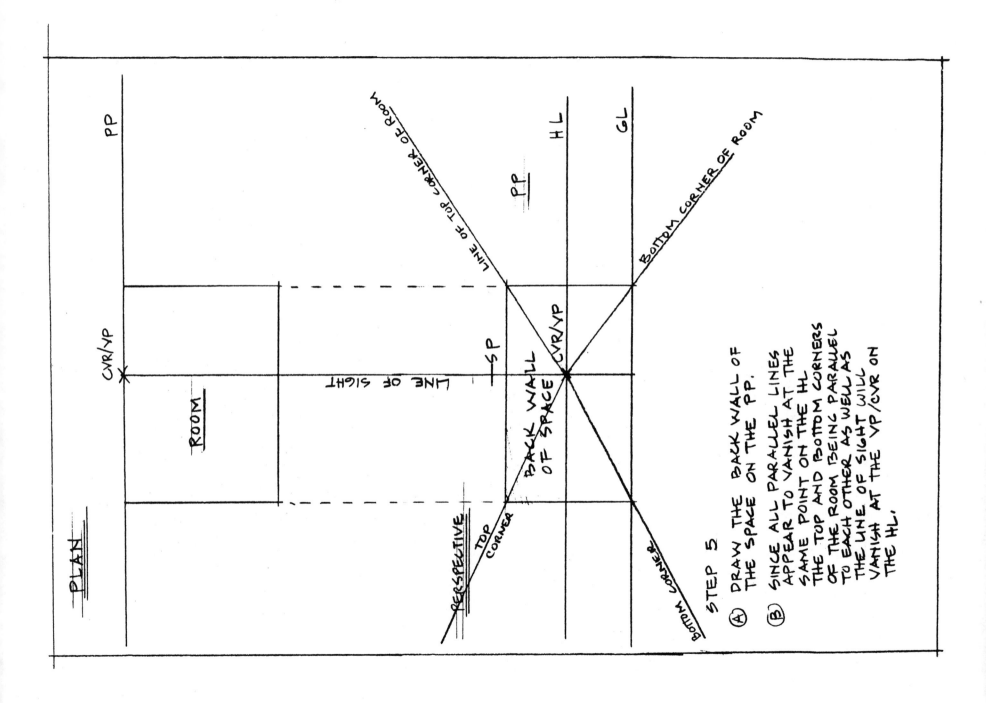

PLAN

PP

CVR/VP

ROOM

LINE OF TOP CORNER OF ROOM

LINE OF SIGHT

SP

PP

HL

GL

CVR/VP

BACK WALL OF SPACE

PERSPECTIVE

TOP CORNER

BOTTOM CORNER OF ROOM

BOTTOM CORNER

STEP 5

Ⓐ DRAW THE BACK WALL OF THE SPACE ON THE PP.

Ⓑ SINCE ALL PARALLEL LINES APPEAR TO VANISH AT THE SAME POINT ON THE HL THE TOP AND BOTTOM CORNERS OF THE ROOM BEING PARALLEL TO EACH OTHER AS WELL AS THE LINE OF SIGHT WILL VANISH AT THE VP/CVR ON THE HL.

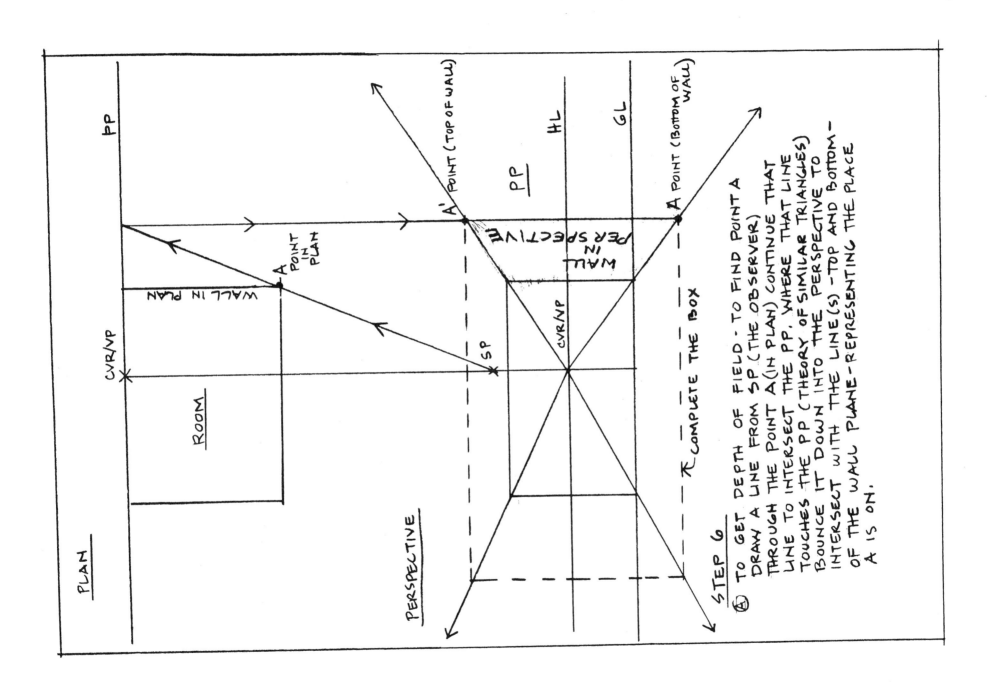

PLAN

PP

CVR/VP

ROOM

WALL IN PLAN

A POINT IN PLAN

SP

PERSPECTIVE

A' (TOP OF WALL)

A' POINT (TOP OF WALL)

PP

HL

GL

WALL IN PERSPECTIVE

CVR/VP

A POINT (BOTTOM OF WALL)

COMPLETE THE BOX

STEP 6

Ⓐ TO GET DEPTH OF FIELD - TO FIND POINT A
DRAW A LINE FROM SP (THE OBSERVER)
THROUGH THE POINT A(IN PLAN) CONTINUE THAT
LINE TO INTERSECT THE PP, WHERE THAT LINE
TOUCHES THE PP (THEORY OF SIMILAR TRIANGLES)
BOUNCE IT DOWN INTO THE PERSPECTIVE TO
INTERSECT WITH THE LINE(S) - TOP AND BOTTOM -
OF THE WALL PLANE - REPRESENTING THE PLACE
A IS ON.

23

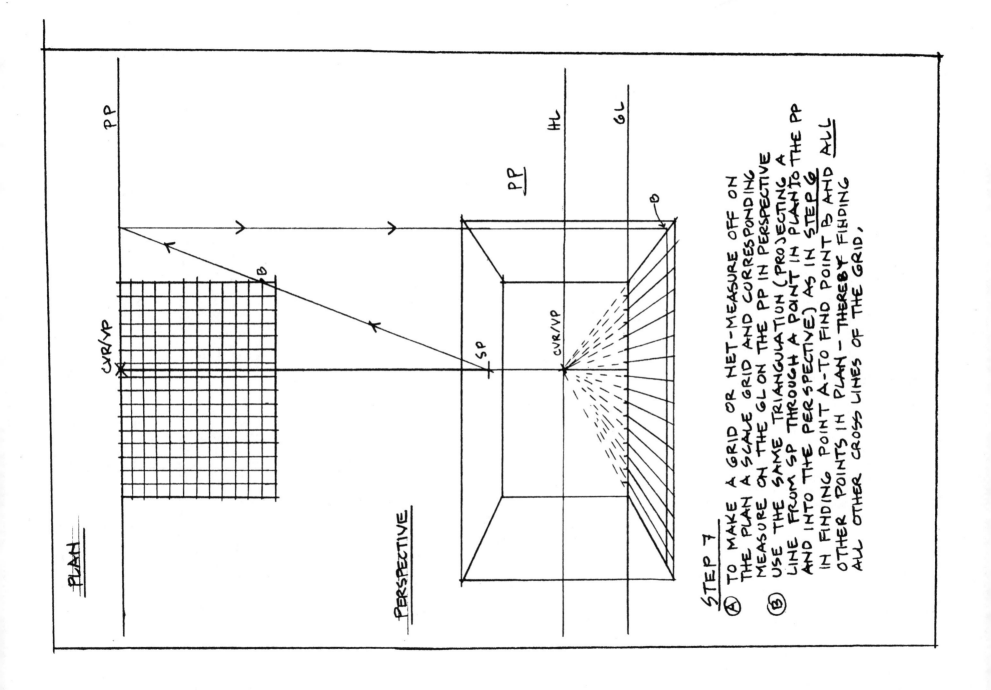

PLAN

PP

CVR/VP

B

PERSPECTIVE

PP

HL

GL

SP

CVR/VP

B

STEP 7

Ⓐ TO MAKE A GRID OR NET-MEASURE OFF ON
THE PLAN A SCALE GRID AND CORRESPONDING
MEASURE ON THE GL ON THE PP IN PERSPECTIVE

Ⓑ USE THE SAME TRIANGULATION (PROJECTING A
LINE FROM SP THROUGH A POINT IN PLAN TO THE PP
AND INTO THE PERSPECTIVE) AS IN STEP 6
IN FINDING POINT A—TO FIND POINT B AND ALL
OTHER POINTS IN PLAN—THEREBY FINDING
ALL OTHER CROSS LINES OF THE GRID.

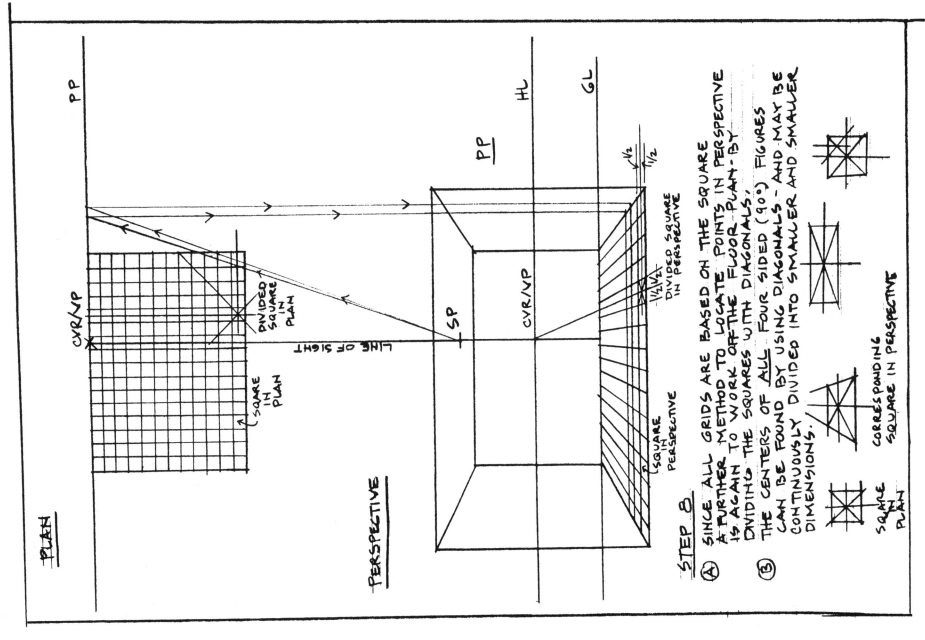

PLAN

PERSPECTIVE

PP

CVR/VP

SQUARE IN PLAN

DIVIDED SQUARE IN PLAN

LINE OF SIGHT

SP

CVR/VP

PP

HL

GL

CVR/VP

SQUARE IN PERSPECTIVE

1/2 1/2

1/2 1/2

DIVIDED SQUARE IN PERSPECTIVE

STEP 8

Ⓐ SINCE ALL GRIDS ARE BASED ON THE SQUARE A FURTHER METHOD TO LOCATE POINTS IN PERSPECTIVE IS AGAIN TO WORK OF THE FLOOR PLAN - BY DIVIDING THE SQUARES WITH DIAGONALS.

Ⓑ THE CENTERS OF ALL FOUR SIDED (90°) FIGURES CAN BE FOUND BY USING DIAGONALS - AND MAY BE CONTINUOUSLY DIVIDED INTO SMALLER AND SMALLER DIMENSIONS.

CORRESPONDING SQUARE IN PERSPECTIVE

SQUARE IN PLAN

25

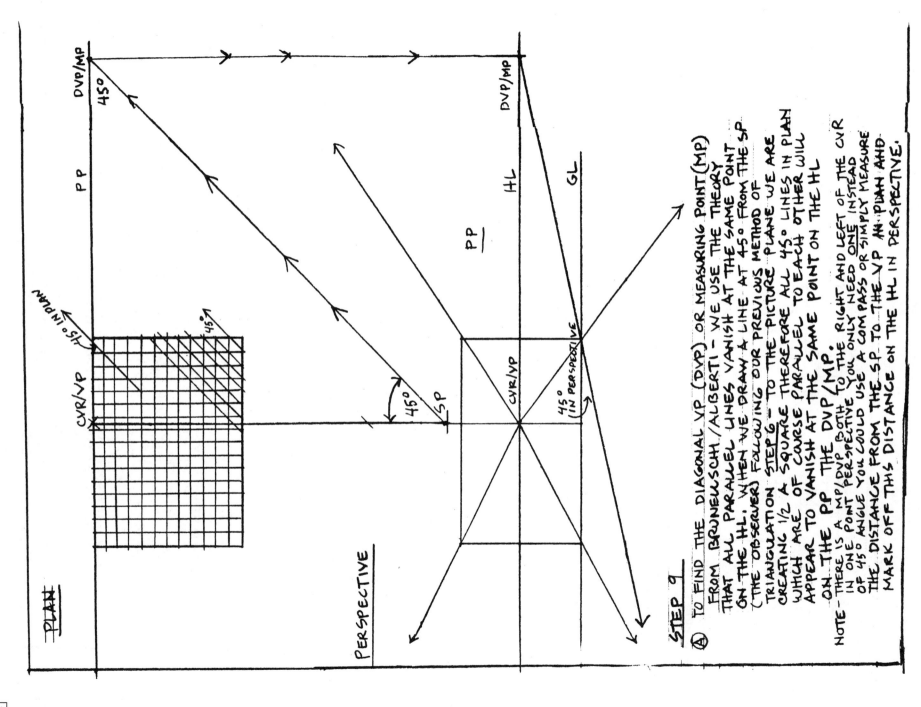

PLAN

DVP/MP

PP

45°

45° in PLAN

CVR/VP

CVR/VP

45°

SP

DVP/MP

PP

HL

GL

PERSPECTIVE

CVR/VP

45°
(IN PERSPECTIVE)

45°
(IN PERSPECTIVE)

STEP 9

Ⓐ TO FIND THE DIAGONAL VP (DVP) OR MEASURING POINT (MP)

FROM BRUNELLESCHI/ALBERTI - WE USE THE THEORY
THAT ALL PARALLEL LINES VANISH AT THE SAME POINT
ON THE HL. WHEN WE DRAW A LINE AT 45° FROM THE SP
("THE OBSERVER") FOLLOWING OUR PREVIOUS METHOD OF
TRIANGULATION STEP 6 - TO THE PICTURE PLANE WE ARE
CREATING ½ A SQUARE THEREFORE ALL 45° LINES IN PLAN
WHICH ARE OF COURSE PARALLEL TO EACH OTHER WILL
APPEAR TO VANISH AT THE SAME POINT ON THE HL
ON THE PP THE DVP/MP.

NOTE - THERE IS A MP/DVP BOTH TO THE RIGHT AND LEFT OF THE CVR
IN ONE POINT PERSPECTIVE YOU ONLY NEED ONE INSTEAD
OF 45° ANGLE YOU COULD USE A COMPASS OR SIMPLY MEASURE
THE DISTANCE FROM THE SP TO THE VP IN PLAN AND
MARK OFF THIS DISTANCE ON THE HL IN PERSPECTIVE.

26

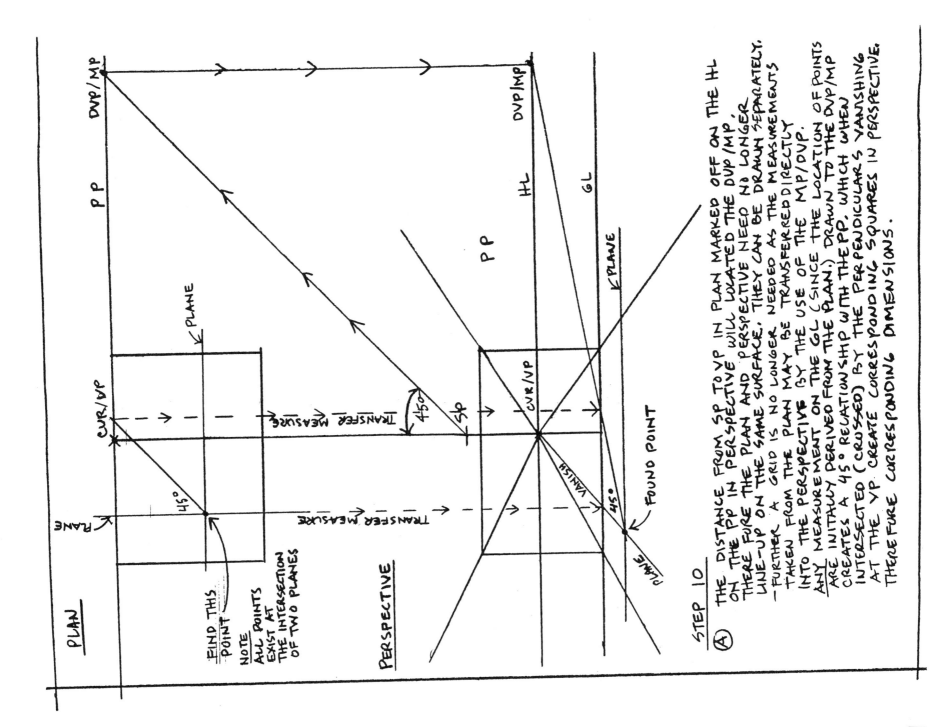

PLAN

FIND THIS POINT

NOTE
ALL POINTS
EXIST AT
THE INTERSECTION
OF TWO PLANES

PLANE

45°

CVR/VP

TRANSFER MEASURE

45°

TRANSFER MEASURE

PLANE

PP

DVP/MP

PERSPECTIVE

PP

CVR/VP

VANISH

45°

FOUND POINT

PLANE

PLANE

SP

HL

DVP/MP

GL

STEP 10

Ⓐ THE DISTANCE FROM SP TO VP IN PLAN MARKED OFF ON THE HL
ON THE PP IN PERSPECTIVE WILL LOCATED THE DVP/MP.
THEREFORE THE PLAN AND PERSPECTIVE NEED NO LONGER
LINE-UP ON THE SAME SURFACE, THEY CAN BE DRAWN SEPARATELY.
FURTHER, A GRID IS NO LONGER NEEDED AS THE MEASUREMENTS
TAKEN FROM THE PLAN MAY BE TRANSFERRED DIRECTLY
INTO THE PERSPECTIVE BY THE USE OF THE MP/DVP.
ANY MEASUREMENT ON THE GL (SINCE THE LOCATION OF POINTS
ARE INITIALLY DERIVED FROM THE PLAN) DRAWN TO THE DVP/MP
CREATES A 45° RELATIONSHIP WITH THE PP, WHICH WHEN
INTERSECTED (CROSSED) BY THE PERPENDICULARS VANISHING
AT THE VP CREATE CORRESPONDING SQUARES IN PERSPECTIVE,
THEREFURE CORRESPONDING DIMENSIONS.

27

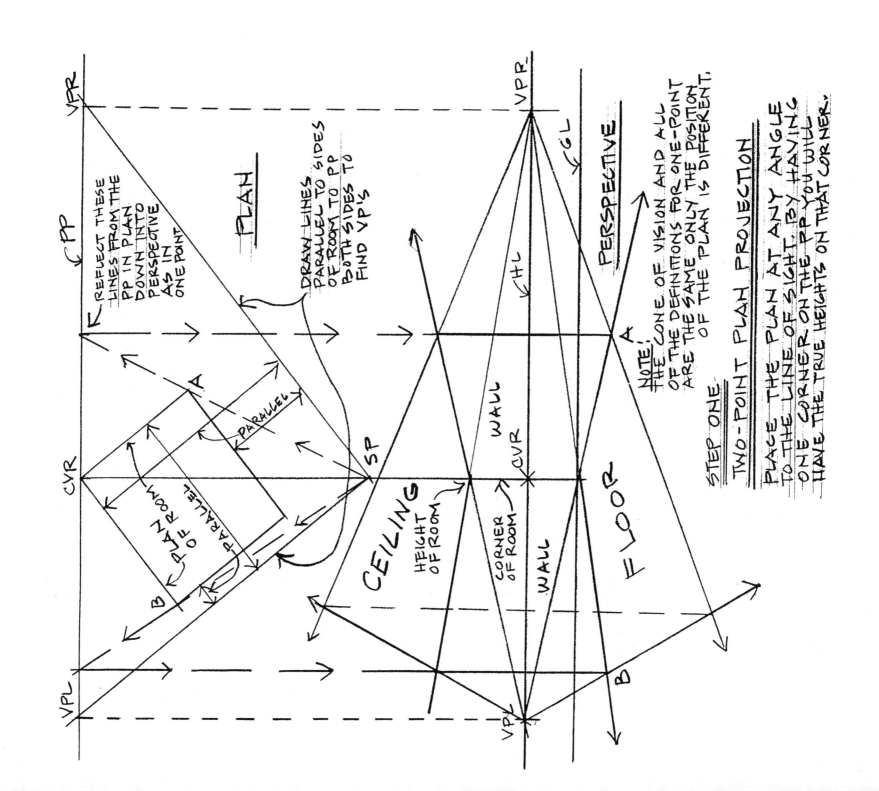

PLAN

REFLECT THESE LINES FROM THE PP IN PLAN DOWN INTO PERSPECTIVE AS IN ONE POINT

DRAW LINES PARALLEL TO SIDES OF ROOM TO PP BOTH SIDES TO FIND VP's

VPR

PP

CVR

PARALLEL

PLAN OF ROOM

PARALLEL

A

B

VPL

SP

VPR

GL

HL

PERSPECTIVE

A

NOTE:
THE CONE OF VISION AND ALL OF THE DEFINITIONS FOR ONE-POINT ARE THE SAME ONLY THE POSITION OF THE PLAN IS DIFFERENT.

STEP ONE

TWO-POINT PLAN PROJECTION

PLACE THE PLAN AT ANY ANGLE TO THE LINE OF SIGHT, BY HAVING ONE CORNER ON THE PP YOU WILL HAVE THE TRUE HEIGHTS ON THAT CORNER.

CEILING
HEIGHT OF ROOM

WALL

CVR

CORNER OF ROOM

WALL

FLOOR

B

VP

28

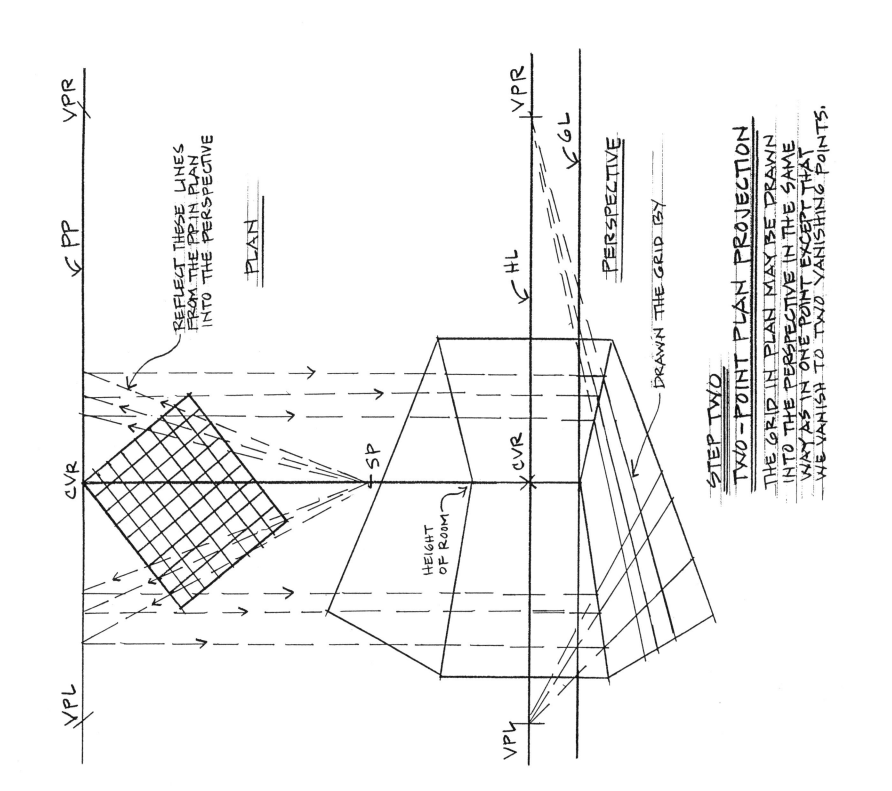

REFLECT THESE LINES FROM THE PLAN INTO THE PERSPECTIVE

PLAN

VPR

PP

CVR

SP

VPL

VPR

HL

GL

CVR

HEIGHT OF ROOM

VPL

PERSPECTIVE

DRAWN THE GRID BY

STEP TWO

TWO-POINT PLAN PROJECTION

THE GRID IN PLAN MAY BE DRAWN INTO THE PERSPECTIVE IN THE SAME WAY AS IN ONE POINT, EXCEPT THAT WE VANISH TO TWO VANISHING POINTS.

MEASURING POINT METHOD
One-Point Perspective and Two-Point Perspective

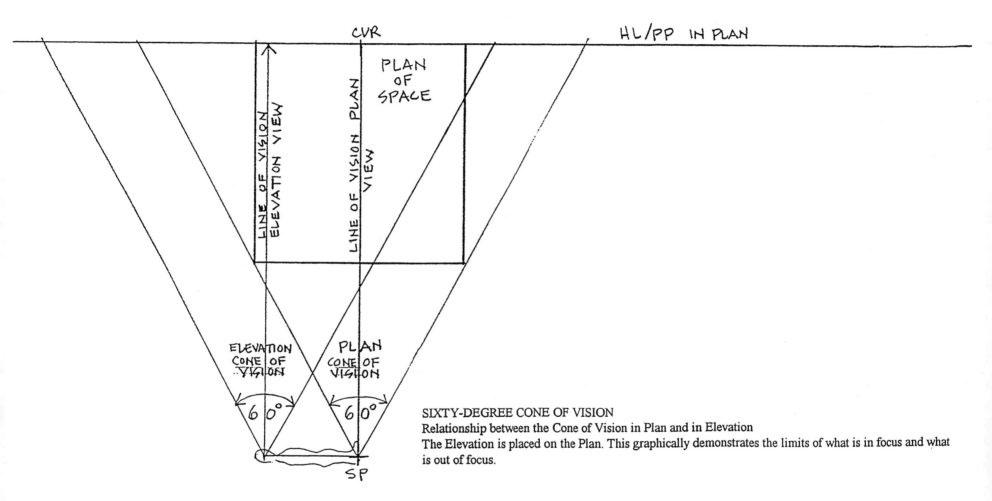

CVR

HL/PP IN PLAN

PLAN
OF
SPACE

LINE OF VISION ELEVATION VIEW

LINE OF VISION PLAN VIEW

ELEVATION CONE OF VISION

PLAN CONE OF VISION

60°   60°

SP

SIXTY-DEGREE CONE OF VISION
Relationship between the Cone of Vision in Plan and in Elevation
The Elevation is placed on the Plan. This graphically demonstrates the limits of what is in focus and what is out of focus.

IN-FOCUS
OUT-OF-FOCUS
Using the 60 degree cone of vision check the location of the observer the SP
in both the plan and the elevation .

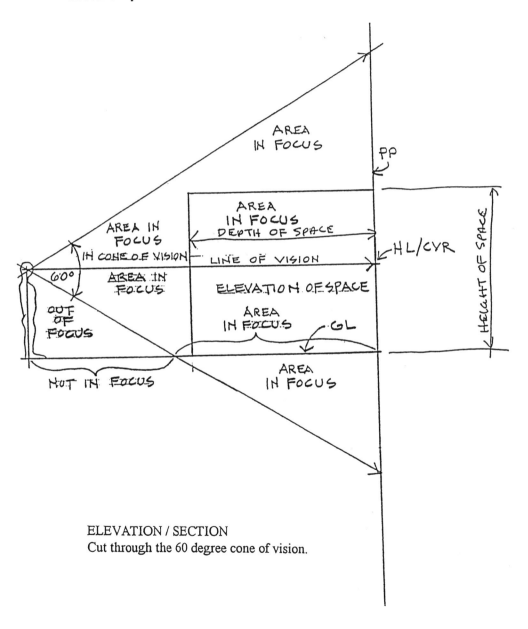

ELEVATION / SECTION
Cut through the 60 degree cone of vision.

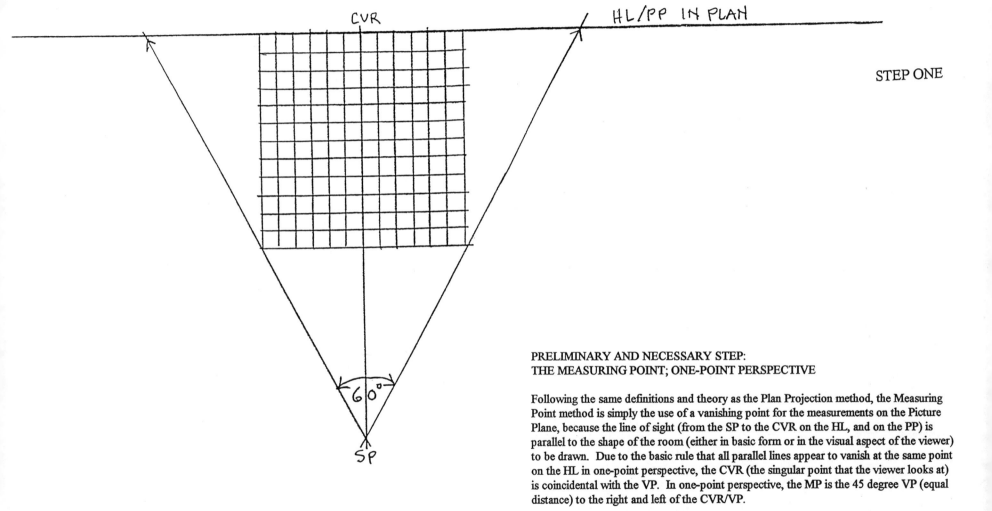

CVR

HL/PP IN PLAN

STEP ONE

60°

SP

PRELIMINARY AND NECESSARY STEP:
THE MEASURING POINT; ONE-POINT PERSPECTIVE

Following the same definitions and theory as the Plan Projection method, the Measuring Point method is simply the use of a vanishing point for the measurements on the Picture Plane, because the line of sight (from the SP to the CVR on the HL, and on the PP) is parallel to the shape of the room (either in basic form or in the visual aspect of the viewer) to be drawn. Due to the basic rule that all parallel lines appear to vanish at the same point on the HL in one-point perspective, the CVR (the singular point that the viewer looks at) is coincidental with the VP. In one-point perspective, the MP is the 45 degree VP (equal distance) to the right and left of the CVR/VP.

With two-point perspective, the two measuring points are also vanishing points and, as in one-point perspective, the relationship between the PP, the SP, and the VP is triangular.

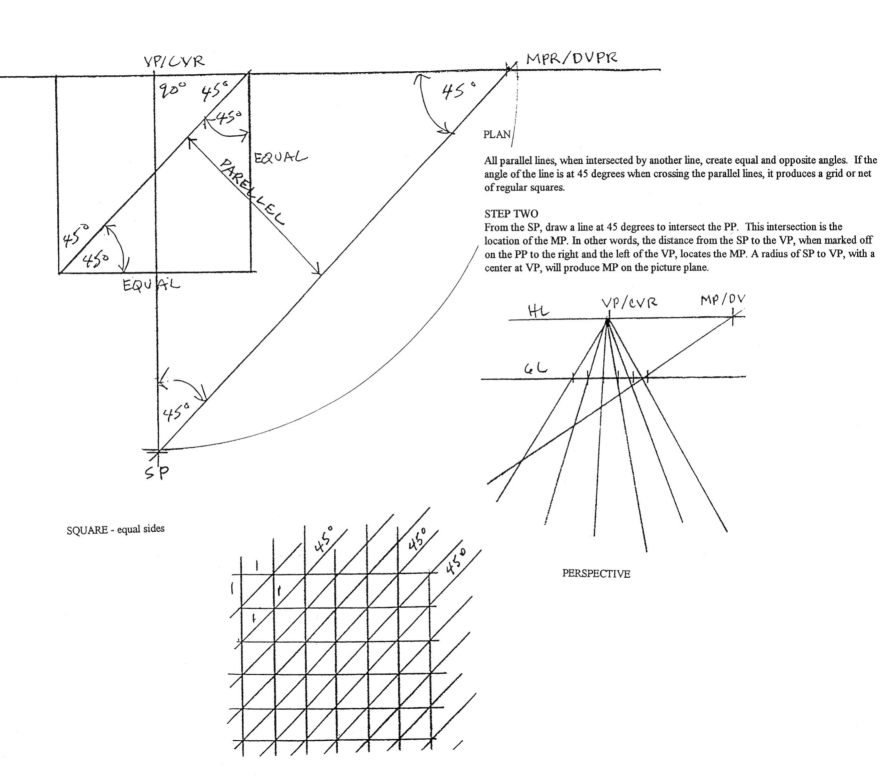

VP/CVR

MPR/DVPR

90°   45°

45°

45°

PARELLEL

EQUAL

45°

45°

EQUAL

45°

45°

SP

PLAN

All parallel lines, when intersected by another line, create equal and opposite angles. If the angle of the line is at 45 degrees when crossing the parallel lines, it produces a grid or net of regular squares.

STEP TWO

From the SP, draw a line at 45 degrees to intersect the PP. This intersection is the location of the MP. In other words, the distance from the SP to the VP, when marked off on the PP to the right and the left of the VP, locates the MP. A radius of SP to VP, with a center at VP, will produce MP on the picture plane.

HL   VP/CVR   MP/DV

GL

PERSPECTIVE

SQUARE - equal sides

45°   45°   45°

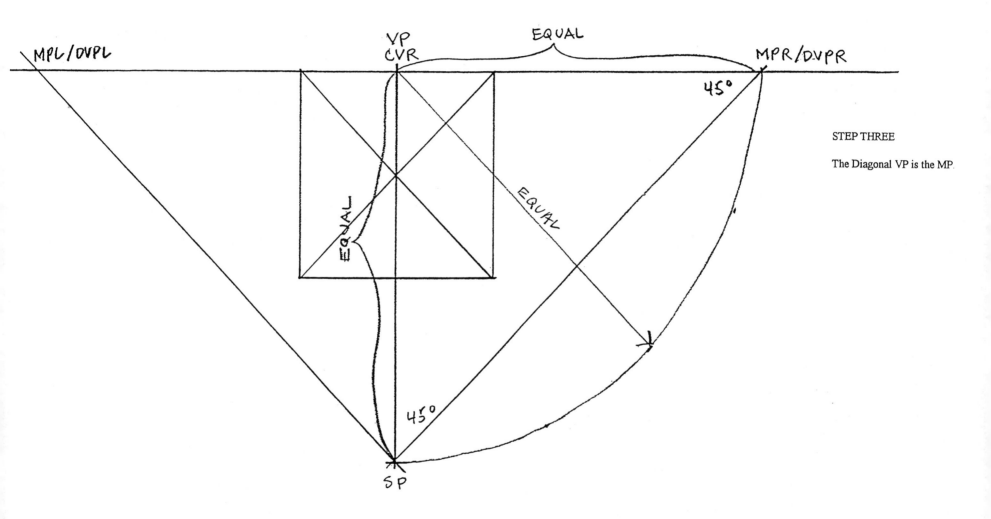

MPL/DVPL

VP
CVR

EQUAL

MPR/DVPR

45°

EQUAL

EQUAL

45°

SP

STEP THREE

The Diagonal VP is the MP.

36

STEP FOUR

On the PP locate the GL, and the HL. On the HL locate the CVR/VP and the MP.
On the PP mark-off measurements on the GL as well as on a vertical line drawn through the CVR/VP

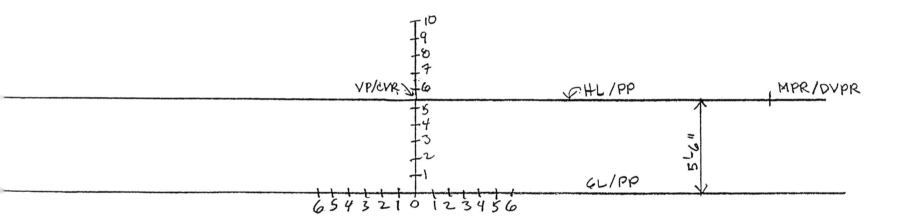

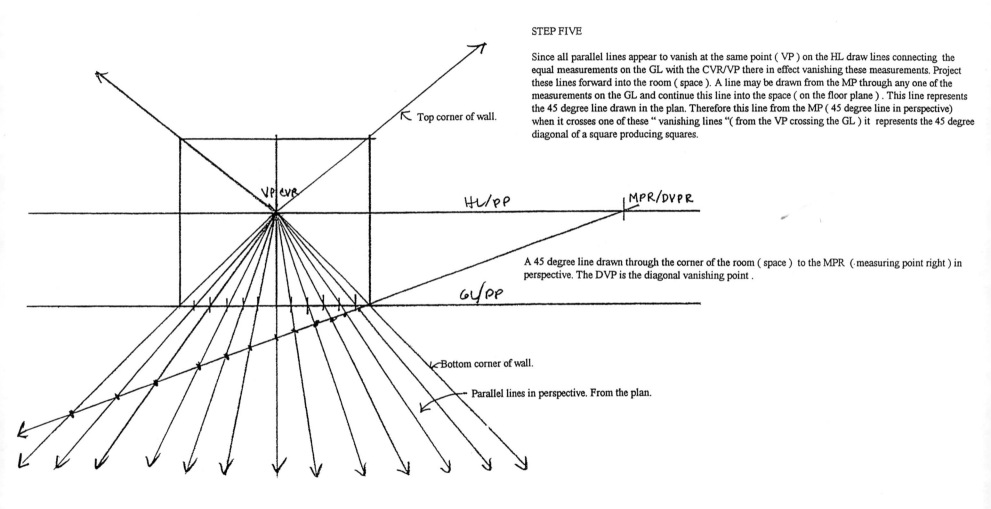

STEP FIVE

Since all parallel lines appear to vanish at the same point (VP) on the HL draw lines connecting the equal measurements on the GL with the CVR/VP there in effect vanishing these measurements. Project these lines forward into the room (space). A line may be drawn from the MP through any one of the measurements on the GL and continue this line into the space (on the floor plane) . This line represents the 45 degree line drawn in the plan. Therefore this line from the MP (45 degree line in perspective) when it crosses one of these " vanishing lines "(from the VP crossing the GL) it represents the 45 degree diagonal of a square producing squares.

Top corner of wall.

VP CVR

HL/PP

MPR/DVPR

A 45 degree line drawn through the corner of the room (space) to the MPR (measuring point right) in perspective. The DVP is the diagonal vanishing point .

GL/PP

Bottom corner of wall.

Parallel lines in perspective. From the plan.

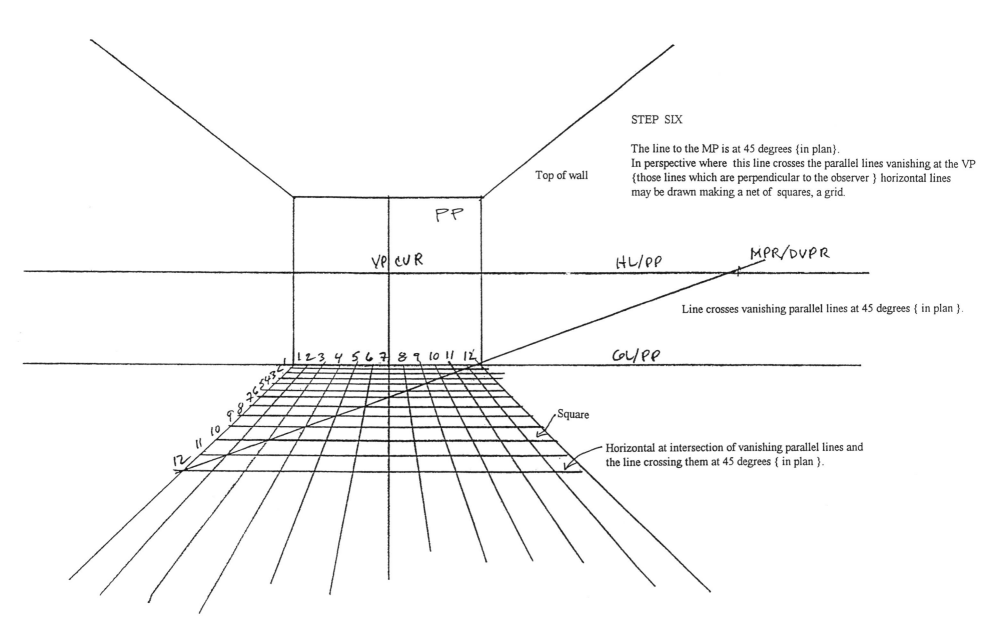

Top of wall

PP

VP CU R

HL/PP

MPR/DVPR

Line crosses vanishing parallel lines at 45 degrees { in plan }.

1 2 3 4 5 6 7 8 9 10 11 12

GL/PP

Square

Horizontal at intersection of vanishing parallel lines and
the line crossing them at 45 degrees { in plan }.

STEP SIX

The line to the MP is at 45 degrees {in plan}.
In perspective where this line crosses the parallel lines vanishing at the VP
{those lines which are perpendicular to the observer } horizontal lines
may be drawn making a net of squares, a grid.

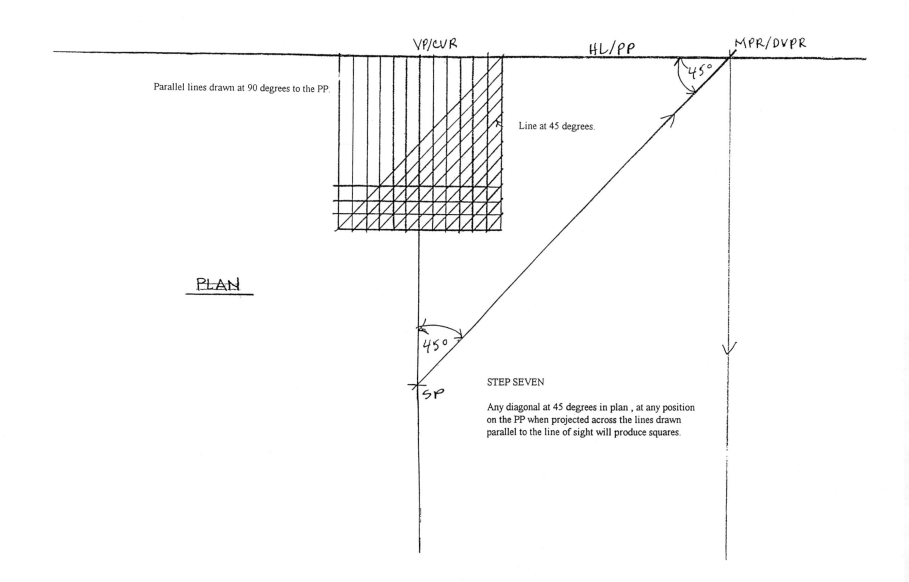

VP/CVR

HL/PP

MPR/DVPR

45°

Parallel lines drawn at 90 degrees to the PP.

Line at 45 degrees.

PLAN

45°

SP

STEP SEVEN

Any diagonal at 45 degrees in plan , at any position
on the PP when projected across the lines drawn
parallel to the line of sight will produce squares.

40

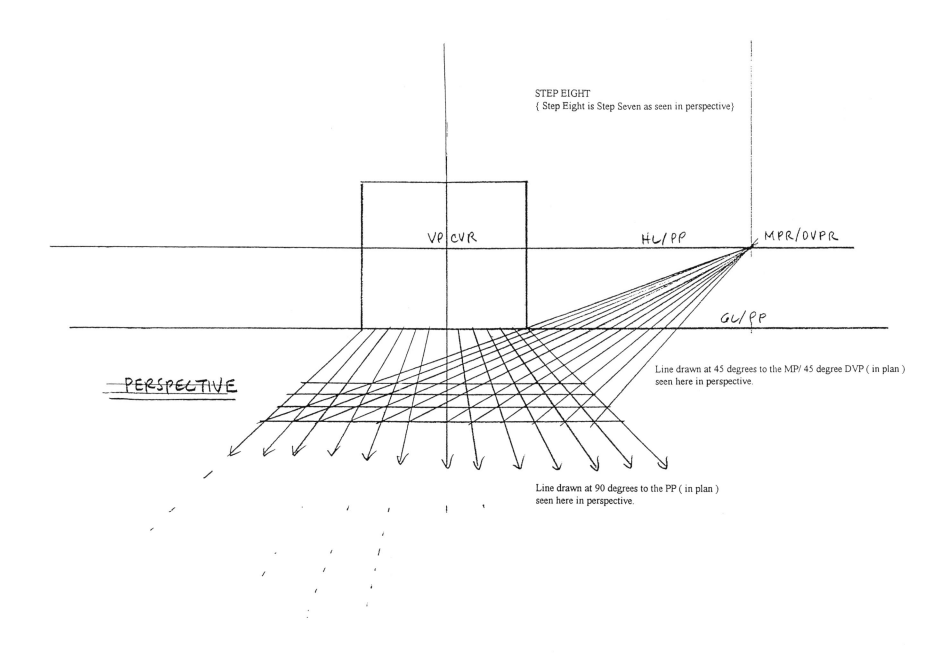

STEP EIGHT
{ Step Eight is Step Seven as seen in perspective}

VP/CVR

HL/PP

MPR/OVPR

GL/PP

PERSPECTIVE

Line drawn at 45 degrees to the MP/ 45 degree DVP (in plan)
seen here in perspective.

Line drawn at 90 degrees to the PP (in plan)
seen here in perspective.

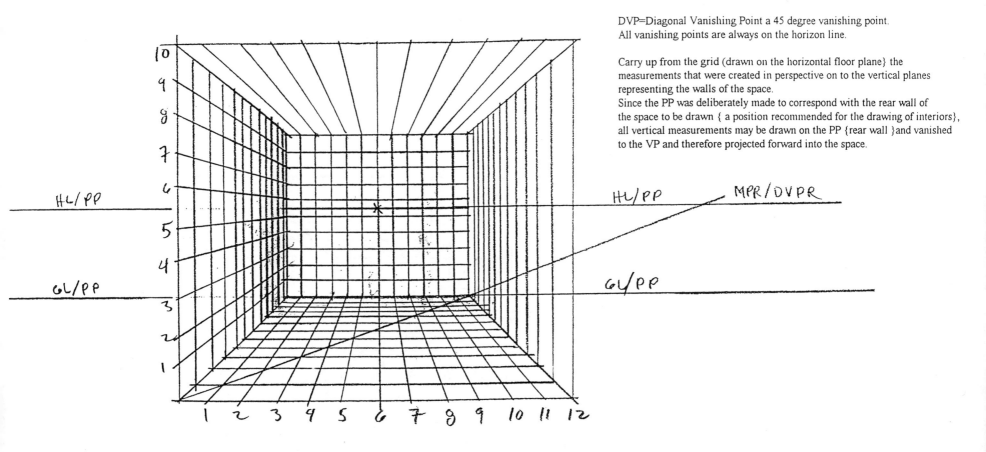

STEP NINE

DVP=Diagonal Vanishing Point a 45 degree vanishing point.
All vanishing points are always on the horizon line.

Carry up from the grid (drawn on the horizontal floor plane} the
measurements that were created in perspective on to the vertical planes
representing the walls of the space.
Since the PP was deliberately made to correspond with the rear wall of
the space to be drawn { a position recommended for the drawing of interiors},
all vertical measurements may be drawn on the PP {rear wall }and vanished
to the VP and therefore projected forward into the space.

HL/PP   HL/PP   MPR/DVPR

GL/PP   GL/PP

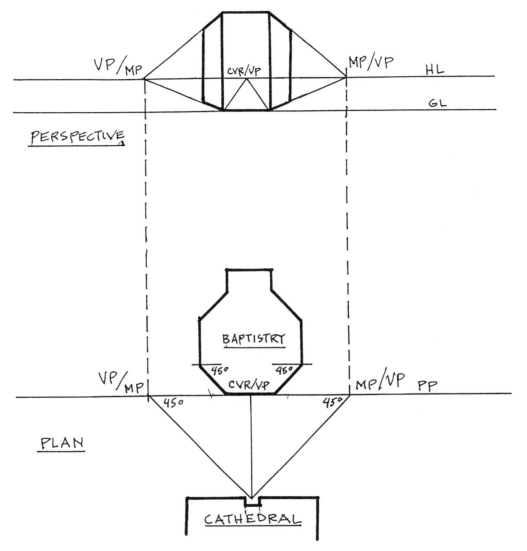

VP/MP   MP/VP   HL

CVR/VP

GL

PERSPECTIVE

BAPTISTRY

45°   45°

VP/MP   CVR/VP   MP/VP   PP

45°   45°

PLAN

CATHEDRAL

BRUNELLESCHI AND THE MEASURING POINT
When Brunelleschi "invented" perspective, he attracted attention and recognition by painting a perspective of the Baptistry from a SP inside the front door of the Cathedral in Florence, Italy. As the Baptistry has 45 degree sides facing the cathedral, a simple diagram of the plan and perspective show that when that famous perspective was made, the 45 degree VP = the MP was used.

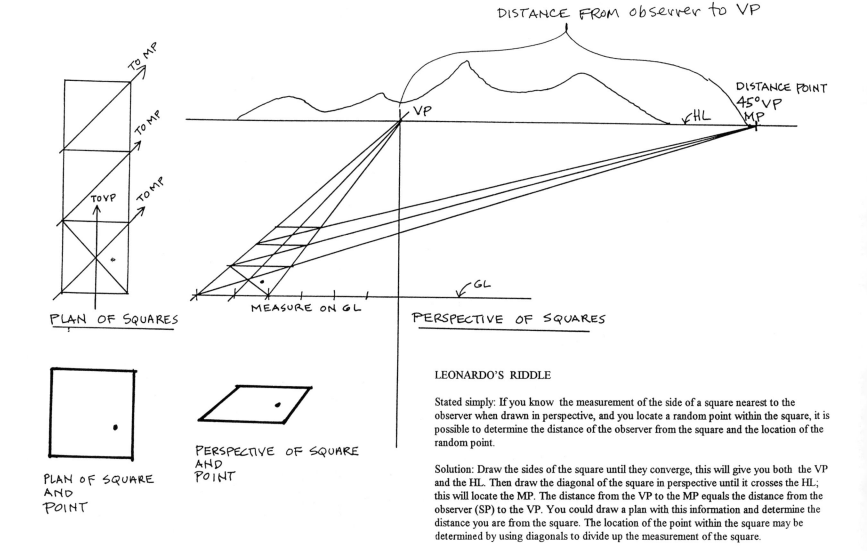

DISTANCE FROM observer to VP

DISTANCE POINT
45° VP
MP

TO MP

TO MP

TO MP

TO VP

TO MP

VP

HL

GL

PLAN OF SQUARES

MEASURE ON GL

PERSPECTIVE OF SQUARES

PLAN OF SQUARE
AND
POINT

PERSPECTIVE OF SQUARE
AND
POINT

LEONARDO'S RIDDLE

Stated simply: If you know the measurement of the side of a square nearest to the observer when drawn in perspective, and you locate a random point within the square, it is possible to determine the distance of the observer from the square and the location of the random point.

Solution: Draw the sides of the square until they converge, this will give you both the VP and the HL. Then draw the diagonal of the square in perspective until it crosses the HL; this will locate the MP. The distance from the VP to the MP equals the distance from the observer (SP) to the VP. You could draw a plan with this information and determine the distance you are from the square. The location of the point within the square may be determined by using diagonals to divide up the measurement of the square.

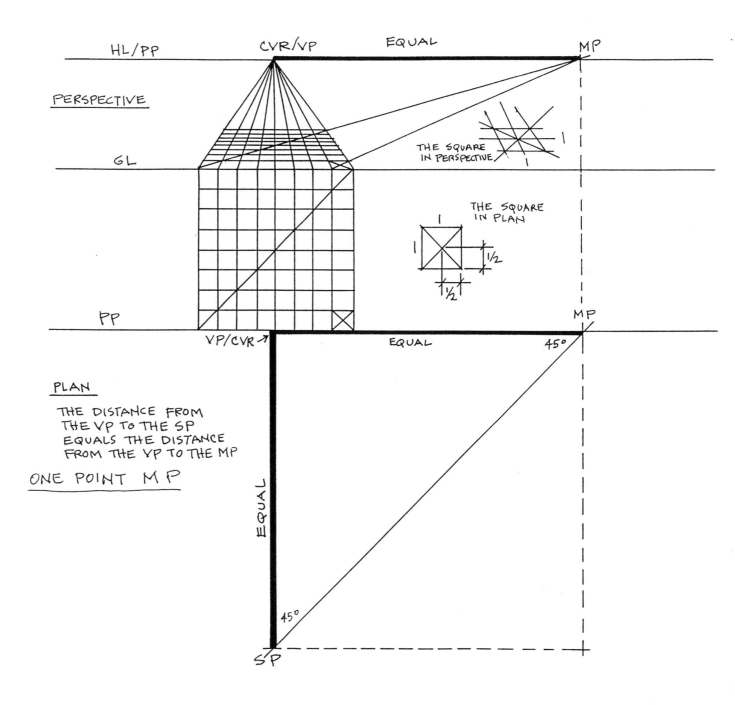

HL/PP   CVR/VP   EQUAL   MP

PERSPECTIVE

THE SQUARE
IN PERSPECTIVE

GL

THE SQUARE
IN PLAN

1

1   ½

                 ½

PP   MP

VP/CVR   EQUAL   45°

PLAN

THE DISTANCE FROM
THE VP TO THE SP
EQUALS THE DISTANCE
FROM THE VP TO THE MP

ONE POINT MP

EQUAL

45°

SP

45

CYR   HL/PP

IN PLAN   ←———— PLAN

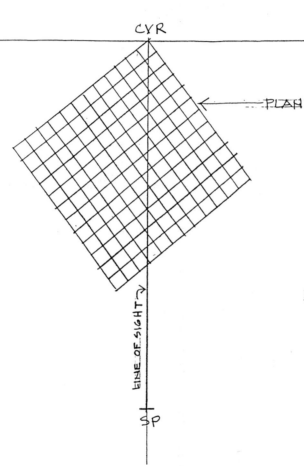

STEP ONE

TWO-POINT PERSPECTIVE
using THE MEASURING POINT

IN PLAN
ROTATE PLAN TO DESIRED ANGLE FOR
VIEWER (IN RELATION TO SP)
PLACE PP TO TOUCH ONE SIDE OR EDGE OF SPACE
PP IS PARALLEL AND PERPENDICULAR TO SP.
FOR MOST INTERIORS PP IS BEST LOCATED AT THE
REAR OR BACK OF SPACE SO AS TO PROJECT
FORWARD (PP CAN BE IN ANY LOCATION)

LINE OF SIGHT

SP

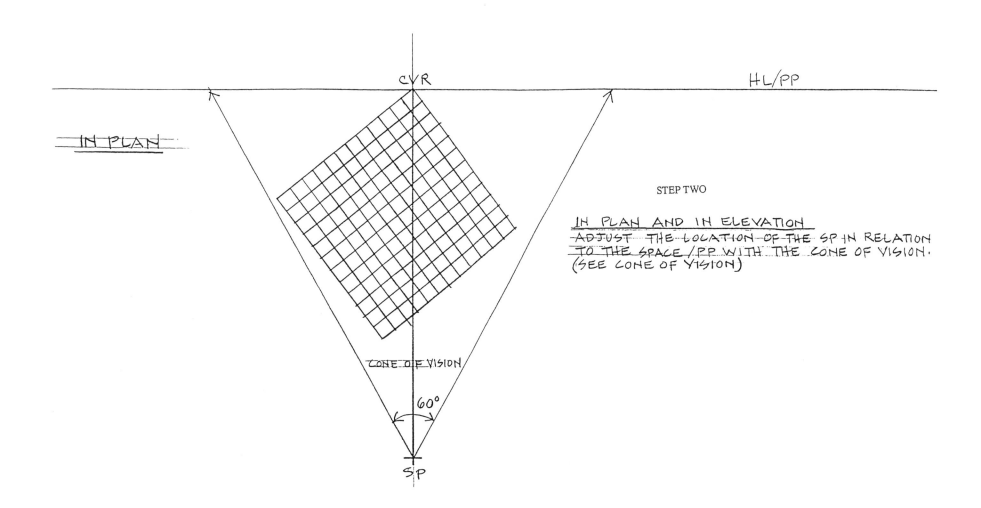

CVR

HL/PP

IN PLAN

STEP TWO

IN PLAN AND IN ELEVATION
ADJUST THE LOCATION OF THE SP IN RELATION
TO THE SPACE / PP WITH THE CONE OF VISION.
(SEE CONE OF VISION)

CONE OF VISION

60°

SP

47

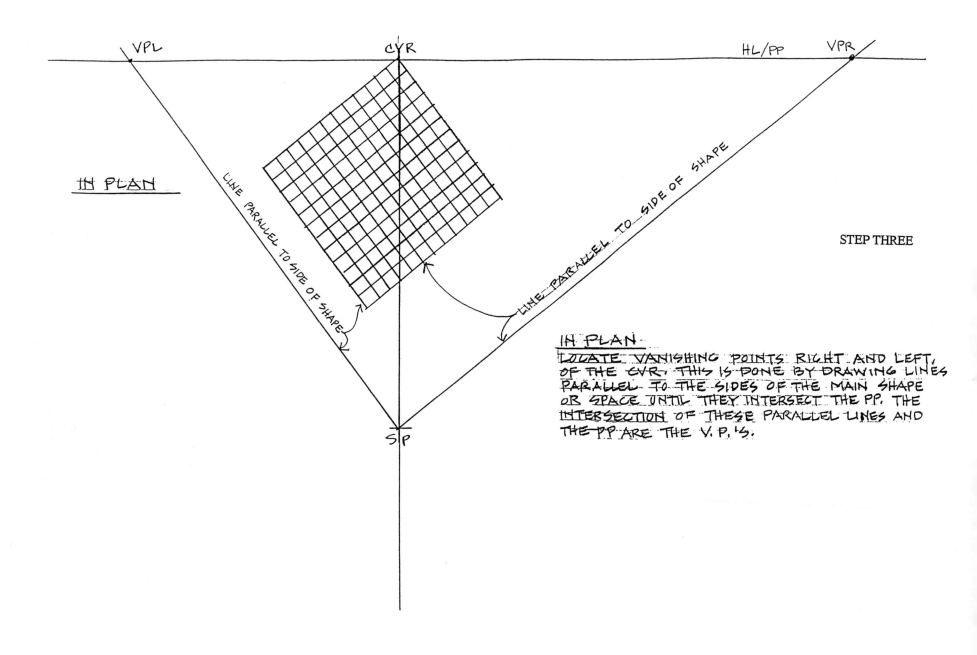

VPL

CVR

HL/PP   VPR

IN PLAN

LINE PARALLEL TO SIDE OF SHAPE

LINE PARALLEL TO SIDE OF SHAPE

STEP THREE

S/P

IN PLAN

LOCATE VANISHING POINTS RIGHT AND LEFT, OF THE CVR. THIS IS DONE BY DRAWING LINES PARALLEL TO THE SIDES OF THE MAIN SHAPE OR SPACE UNTIL THEY INTERSECT THE P.P. THE INTERSECTION OF THESE PARALLEL LINES AND THE P.P. ARE THE V.P.'S.

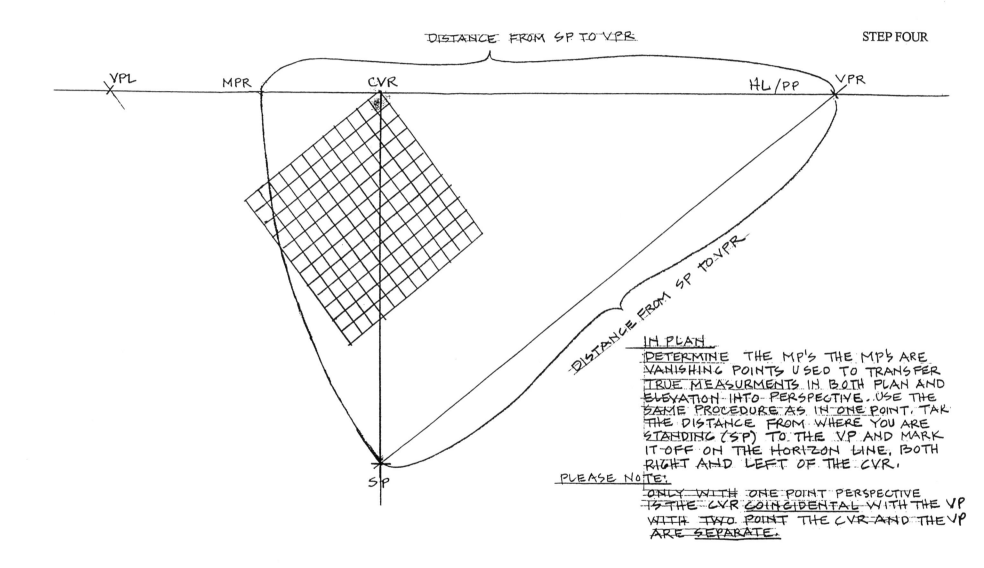

DISTANCE FROM SP TO VPR

VPL   MPR   CVR   HL/PP   VPR

DISTANCE FROM SP TO VPR

SP

IN PLAN

DETERMINE THE MP's THE MP's ARE
VANISHING POINTS USED TO TRANSFER
TRUE MEASURMENTS IN BOTH PLAN AND
ELEVATION INTO PERSPECTIVE. USE THE
SAME PROCEDURE AS IN ONE POINT. TAK
THE DISTANCE FROM WHERE YOU ARE
STANDING (SP) TO THE V.P AND MARK
IT OFF ON THE HORIZON LINE, BOTH
RIGHT AND LEFT OF THE CVR.

PLEASE NOTE:

ONLY WITH ONE POINT PERSPECTIVE
IS THE CVR COINCIDENTAL WITH THE VP
WITH TWO POINT THE CVR AND THE VP
ARE SEPARATE.

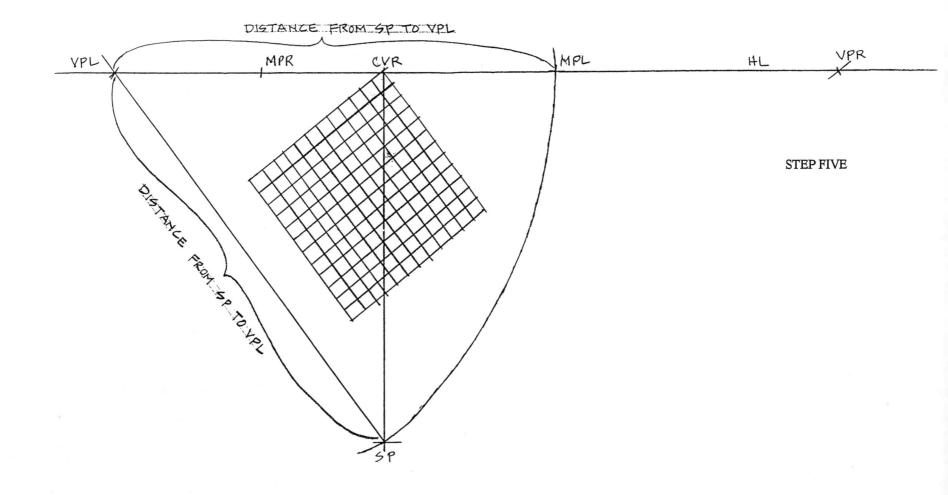

DISTANCE FROM SP TO VPL

VPL   MPR   CVR   MPL   HL   VPR

DISTANCE FROM SP TO VPL

SP

STEP FIVE

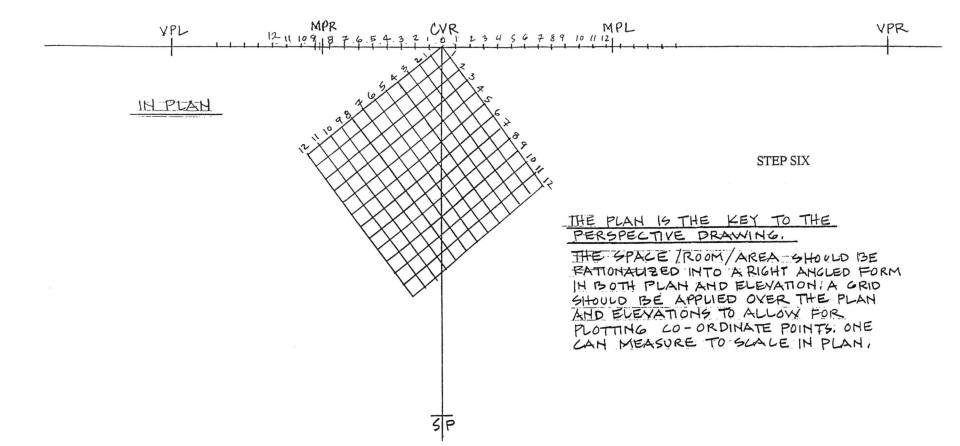

VPL   MPR   CVR   MPL   VPR

12 11 10 9 8 7 6 5 4 3 2 1 0 1 2 3 4 5 6 7 8 9 10 11 12

IN PLAN

STEP SIX

S|P

THE PLAN IS THE KEY TO THE
PERSPECTIVE DRAWING.

THE SPACE / ROOM / AREA SHOULD BE
RATIONALIZED INTO A RIGHT ANGLED FORM
IN BOTH PLAN AND ELEVATION; A GRID
SHOULD BE APPLIED OVER THE PLAN
AND ELEVATIONS TO ALLOW FOR
PLOTTING CO-ORDINATE POINTS. ONE
CAN MEASURE TO SCALE IN PLAN.

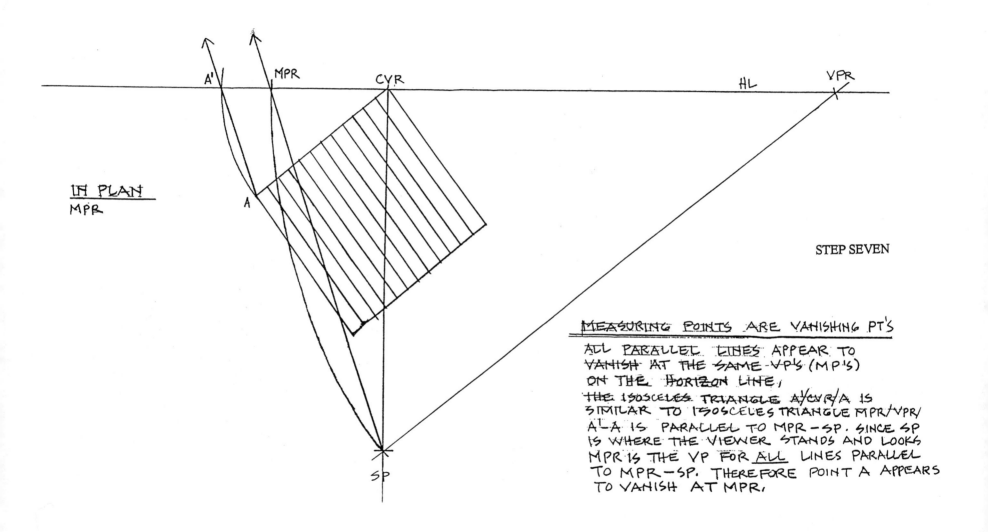

A'

MPR

CVR

HL

VPR

IN PLAN
MPR

A

STEP SEVEN

SP

<u>MEASURING POINTS ARE VANISHING PT'S</u>
ALL <u>PARALLEL</u> <u>LINES</u> APPEAR TO
~~VANISH~~ AT THE SAME ~~VP'S~~ (MP's)
ON THE ~~HORIZON LINE,~~
~~THE ISOSCELES TRIANGLE A'/CVR/A IS~~
~~SIMILAR TO ISOSCELES TRIANGLE MPR/VPR/~~
A'-A IS PARALLEL TO MPR-SP. SINCE SP
IS WHERE THE VIEWER STANDS AND LOOKS
MPR IS THE VP FOR <u>ALL</u> LINES PARALLEL
TO MPR—SP. THEREFORE POINT A APPEARS
TO VANISH AT MPR,

Example- to locate 6 feet in perspective. Measure 6 feet on the PP in plan and draw a line parallel to SP-MPL. Where this line intersects the line representing the bottom corner of the right wall of the room, represents the projected location of 6 feet in plan.

All parallel lines appear to vanish at the same point on the HL. The point to which these parallel lines vanish is a vanishing point.

CVR = where the observer is looking.

6 feet on the PP is the VP for 6 feet in the plan of the room since a line drawn between them is parallel to SP-MPL. This line therefore vanishes at the MPL.

VPL   MPR   CVR   6'   9'   MPL   HL/PP   VPR

A triangle is created with apexes at SP , VPL, and MPL. This triangle has two equal sides, VPL-SP=VPL-MPL, the base of this triangle SP-MPL locates the VP called MPL. Since all parallel lines appear to vanish at the same point on the HL, and similar triangles have equal angles, any measurement on the PP can be projected into perspective, {in front of the PP or behind the PP } by vanishing the dimension { parallel to SP-MPL in plan } from its location on the PP to the MPL.

IN PLAN
MPL

STEP EIGHT

MPL ON THE RIGHT SIDE OF CVR
EXAMPLE / POINTS 6 AND 9 ARE
TRANSFERRED TO THE HORIZON LINE
WITH A COMPASS MAKING ISOSCELES
TRIANGLES LINES 6/6', 9/9' (AND ALL
OTHER POINTS FROM 0 TO 12) ARE
PARALLEL TO LINE SP/MPL.

SP

53

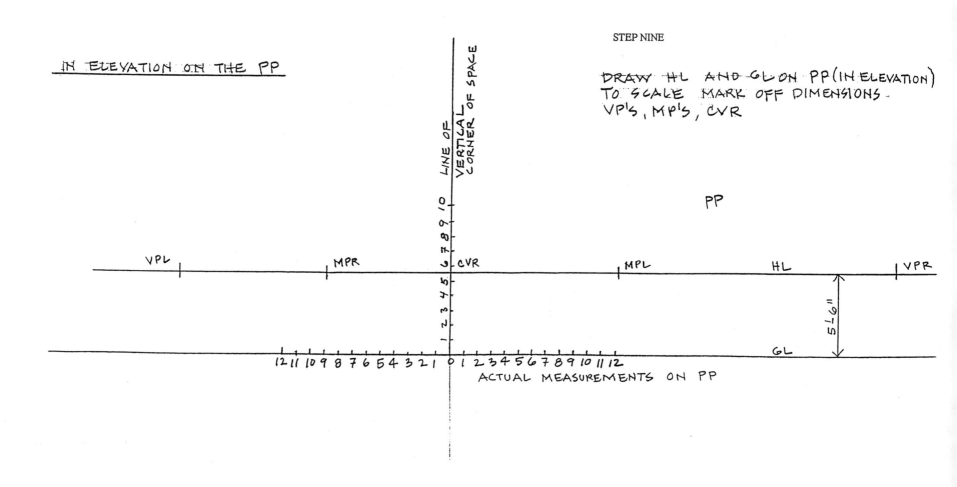

IN ELEVATION ON THE PP

LINE OF
VERTICAL
CORNER OF SPACE

STEP NINE

DRAW HL AND GL ON PP (IN ELEVATION)
TO SCALE MARK OFF DIMENSIONS.
VP's, MP's, CVR

PP

VPL   MPR   CVR   MPL   HL   VPR

5'-6"

GL

12 11 10 9 8 7 6 5 4 3 2 1 0 1 2 3 4 5 6 7 8 9 10 11 12

ACTUAL MEASUREMENTS ON PP

STEP TEN

DRAW LINES THROUGH CORNERS (FLOOR
AND CEILING) OF SPACE FROM VPIS. THROUGH
THE BASE OF THE HT LINE WHERE IT INTERSECTS
THE GL AT O. AND AT THE TOP CORNER
OF THE ROOM AT POINT 10 ON THE HT. LINE,

IN PERSPECTIVE
TOP AND BOTTOM CORNERS OF SPACE

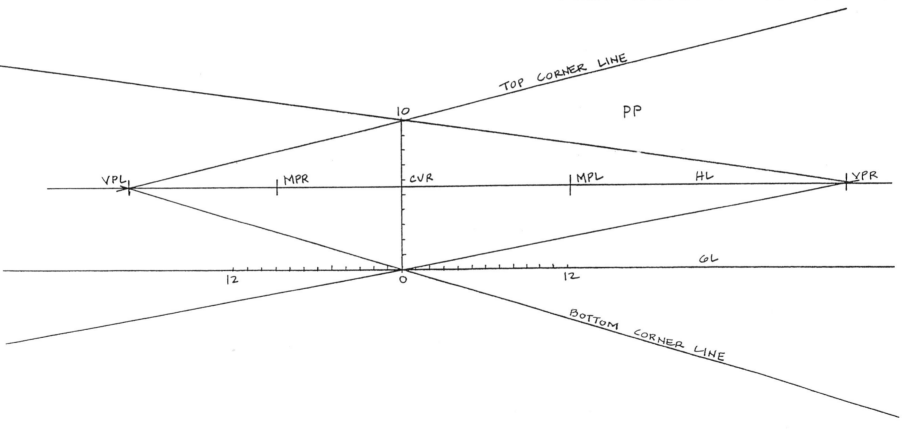

IN PERSPECTIVE

TRANSFER MEASUREMENTS
ON P.P INTO PERSPECTIVE ON
BOTTOM CORNERS OF SPACE

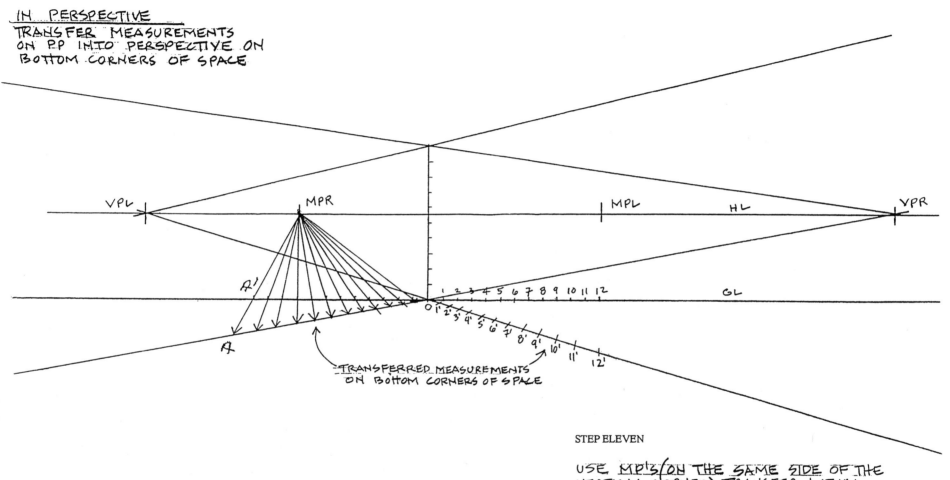

TRANSFERRED MEASUREMENTS
ON BOTTOM CORNERS OF SPACE

STEP ELEVEN

USE MP's (ON THE SAME SIDE OF THE
VERTICAL CORNER) TRANSFER ACTUAL
MEASUREMENTS INTO PERSPECTIVE.
MP's ARE VP's FOR THE TRUE MEASUREMENTS
ON THE GL ON THE P.P.
BRING THE ACTUAL MEASUREMENTS ON THE PP
FORWARD TO THE BOTTOM CORNERS OF THE SPACE

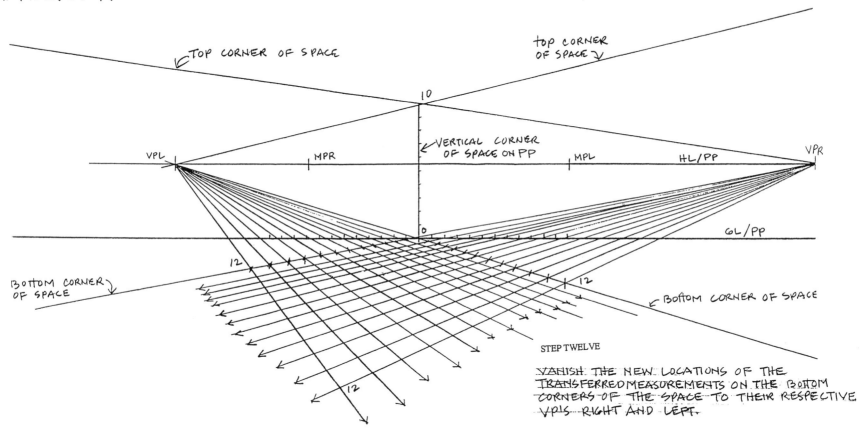

IN PERSPECTIVE
IN FRONT OF P.P.

TOP CORNER OF SPACE

top CORNER OF SPACE

10

VERTICAL CORNER
OF SPACE ON PP

VPL   MPR   MPL   HL/PP   VPR

0   GL/PP

12   12

BOTTOM CORNER
OF SPACE

BOTTOM CORNER OF SPACE

STEP TWELVE

12

VANISH THE NEW LOCATIONS OF THE
TRANSFERRED MEASUREMENTS ON THE BOTTOM
CORNERS OF THE SPACE TO THEIR RESPECTIVE
VP'S RIGHT AND LEFT.

PERSPECTIVE BEHIND THE PICTURE PLANE

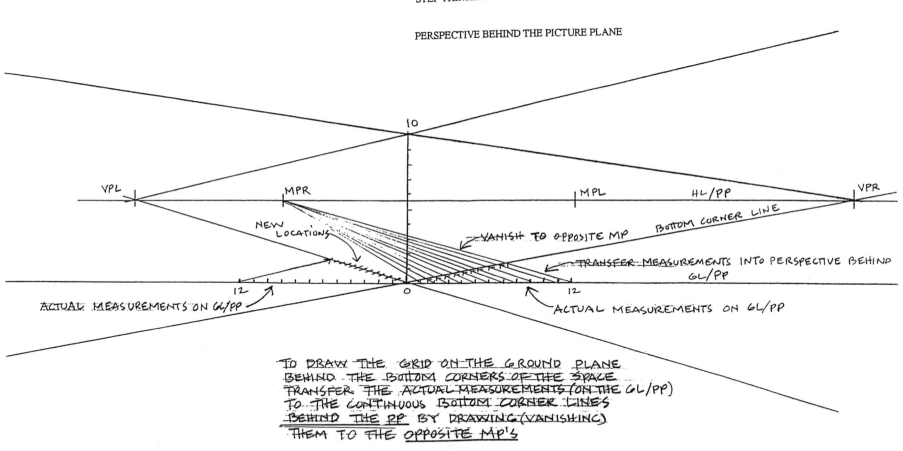

VPL

MPR

NEW
LOCATIONS

VANISH TO OPPOSITE MP

BOTTOM CORNER LINE

MPL

HL/PP

VPR

TRANSFER MEASUREMENTS INTO PERSPECTIVE BEHIND
GL/PP

10

12

0

12

ACTUAL MEASUREMENTS ON GL/PP

ACTUAL MEASUREMENTS ON GL/PP

TO DRAW THE GRID ON THE GROUND PLANE
BEHIND THE BOTTOM CORNERS OF THE SPACE
TRANSFER THE ACTUAL MEASUREMENTS (ON THE GL/PP)
TO THE CONTINUOUS BOTTOM CORNER LINES
BEHIND THE PP BY DRAWING (VANISHING)
THEM TO THE OPPOSITE MP'S

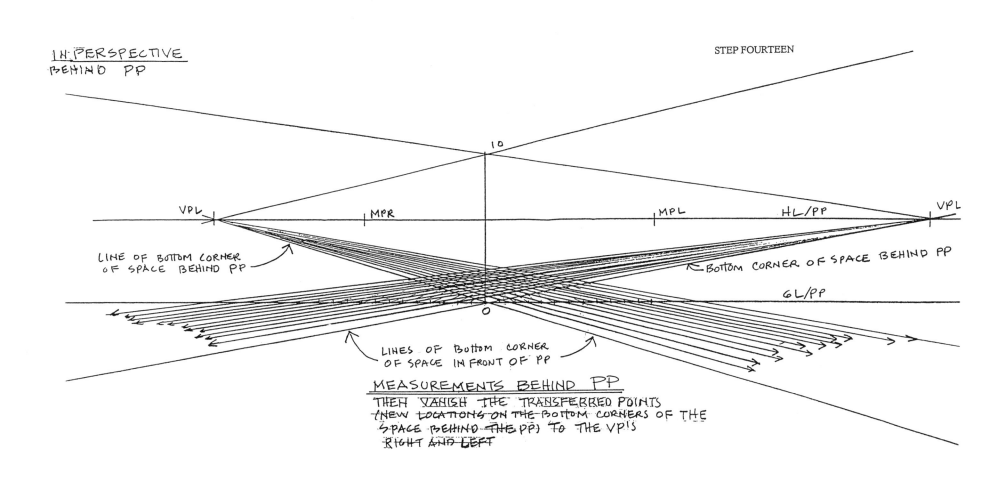

IN PERSPECTIVE
BEHIND PP

10

VPL   MPR   MPL   HL/PP   VPL

LINE OF BOTTOM CORNER
OF SPACE BEHIND PP

BOTTOM CORNER OF SPACE BEHIND PP

GL/PP

O

LINES OF BOTTOM CORNER
OF SPACE IN FRONT OF PP

MEASUREMENTS BEHIND PP
THEN VANISH THE TRANSFERRED POINTS
(NEW LOCATIONS ON THE BOTTOM CORNERS OF THE
SPACE BEHIND THE PP) TO THE VP'S
RIGHT AND LEFT

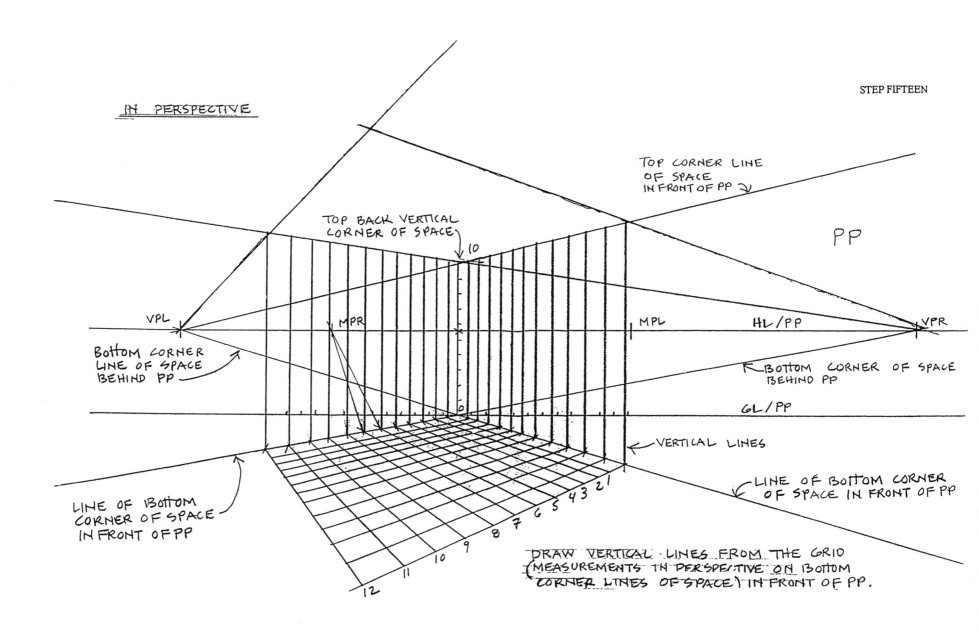

IN PERSPECTIVE

TOP CORNER LINE
OF SPACE
IN FRONT OF PP ↓

PP

TOP BACK VERTICAL
CORNER OF SPACE

10

VPL

MPR

MPL

HL/PP

VPR

BOTTOM CORNER
LINE OF SPACE
BEHIND PP

BOTTOM CORNER OF SPACE
BEHIND PP

0

GL/PP

VERTICAL LINES

LINE OF BOTTOM
CORNER OF SPACE
IN FRONT OF PP

LINE OF BOTTOM CORNER
OF SPACE IN FRONT OF PP

5 4 3 2 1

6

7

8

9

10

11

12

DRAW VERTICAL LINES FROM THE GRID
(MEASUREMENTS IN PERSPECTIVE ON BOTTOM
CORNER LINES OF SPACE) IN FRONT OF PP.

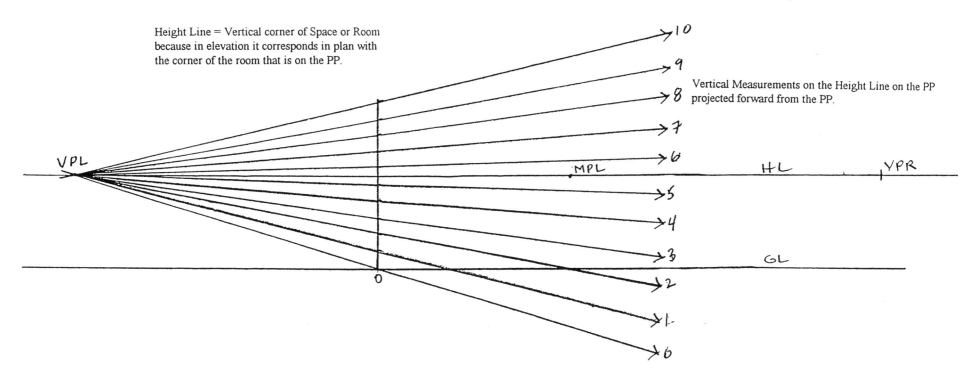

Height Line = Vertical corner of Space or Room because in elevation it corresponds in plan with the corner of the room that is on the PP.

Vertical Measurements on the Height Line on the PP projected forward from the PP.

VPL

MPL

HL

VPR

GL

0

10
9
8
7
6
5
4
3
2
1.
0

STEP SIXTEEN

Measure vertically on the PP { the height line on the corner of the room } and vanish to respective vanishing points to the right and left .
Please note that on this page for clarity only the vertical measurements vanishing to the VPL are shown , those measurements to the VPR should also be drawn.

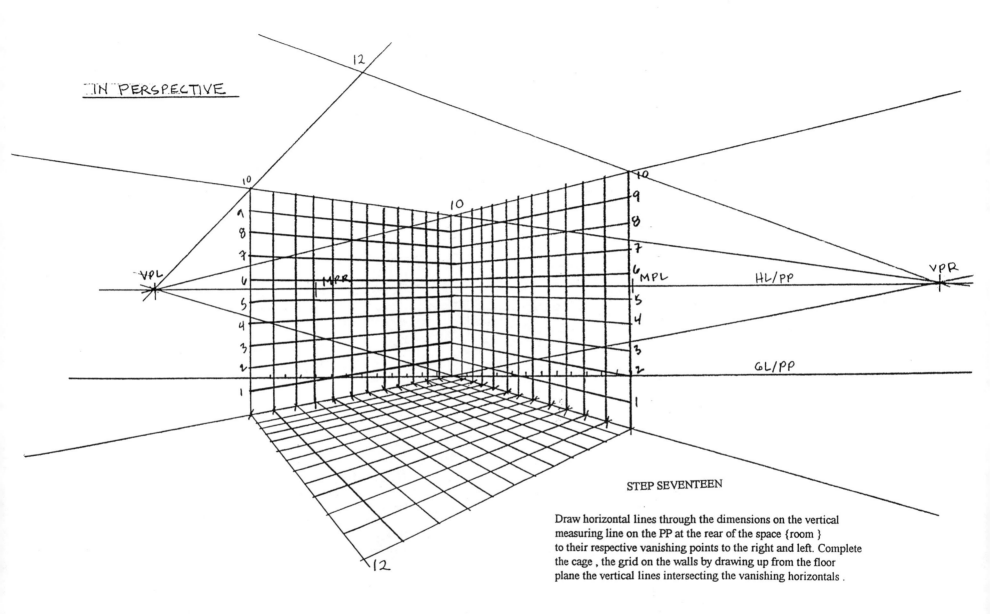

IN PERSPECTIVE

12

10

10

7
8
7
VPL
6   MPR   6 MPL   HL/PP   VPR
5   5
4   4
3   3
2   2   GL/PP
1   1

12

STEP SEVENTEEN

Draw horizontal lines through the dimensions on the vertical
measuring line on the PP at the rear of the space {room }
to their respective vanishing points to the right and left. Complete
the cage , the grid on the walls by drawing up from the floor
plane the vertical lines intersecting the vanishing horizontals .

DEMONSTRATION

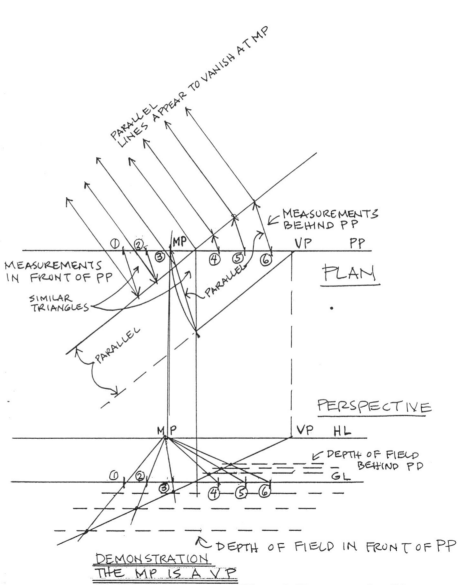

PARALLEL LINES APPEAR TO VANISH AT MP

① ② ③ MP ④ ⑤ ⑥ VP PP

MEASUREMENTS BEHIND PP

MEASUREMENTS IN FRONT OF PP

PLAN

SIMILAR TRIANGLES

PARALLEL

PARALLEL

PERSPECTIVE

M P VP HL

DEPTH OF FIELD BEHIND PD

GL

① ② ③ ④ ⑤ ⑥

DEPTH OF FIELD IN FRONT OF PP

DEMONSTRATION
THE MP IS A VP

DEPTH OF FIELD BOTH IN FRONT OF THE PP
AND BEHIND THE PP IS A DIRECT RESULT OF
THE USE OF SIMILAR TRIANGLES AND
THE PRINCIPLE OF PARALLEL LINES VANISHING
AT THE SAME VP.

FURNITURE/OBJECTS

FURNITURE AND OBJECTS

The process for drawing furniture in perspective is identical to that for drawing all other objects in perspective. The following problem and process reveal the steps needed to draw furniture. The same steps can be applied to add further detail (rugs, lamps, paintings) to this or any other drawing.

PROBLEM:
Create a room drawn at 1/2 of one inch equals one foot. (NOTE: This is good scale for drawing interiors.) The overall aspect of viewing the room is to be one-point. Include two chairs: one chair is in one-point aspect to the observer, and the other chair is in two-point aspect.

PROCESS:
1. Draw the plan and elevation of the rooms, and the plans and elevations of the chairs.

2. In the plan place the PP at the rear of the room. Locate a place to look = CVR, and pull back in a straight line at 90 degrees to the PP, using the 60 degree cone of vision to locate the SP.

3. Choose either plan projection or measuring point method of projection; both methods are interchangeable. To find the MP in one-point perspective, take the distance from where the observer stands = SP to the VP and mark this distance on the HL from the VP in plan. This MP is the 45 degree diagonal VP.

4. Using the information from the plans and elevations of the furniture, plot the points. Project the points from the plan into perspective in order to locate the "footprint" of the chairs. Measure on the PP the measurements (the width and depth), using the MP to get depth of field and the VP to draw those lines that are perpendicular to the PP. All objects and furniture are first drawn as boxes, to ensure that both the form and the aspect are clear.

5. Measure on the PP the heights taken from the elevations of the chairs. (Remember, the PP is the only place possible to measure with a scale in perspective.)

6. Project these height measurements into the perspective along either the planes on which they exist or on the planes that represent the sides of the room; then draw a line across the space to the corresponding point in plan.

7. Draw the lines to the respective VP's. Complete the furniture in a box-like manner first, then adding details as desired. Shades, shadows, and textures as well as adjusted line weights will greatly enhance the drawing, but only after the structure of the perspective is solid and clear.

THE GRID OR NET - 90° SQUARES

THE PLANS AND ELEVATIONS CAN BE PLACED UNDER A GRID OR NET.
THIS HAS BEEN USED IN ANCIENT EGYPTIAN ART TO TRANSFER
GRAPHIC RELATIONSHIPS, A SERIES OF REFERENCE COORDINATES.
BOTH THE LEVEL OF ACCURACY AS WELL AS THE DEGREE OF DETAIL
CAN BE INCREASED BY MAGNIFYING THE GRID. THE MORE REFERENCE
COORDINATES - THE MORE INFORMATION - THE MORE DETAIL AND ACCURACY.

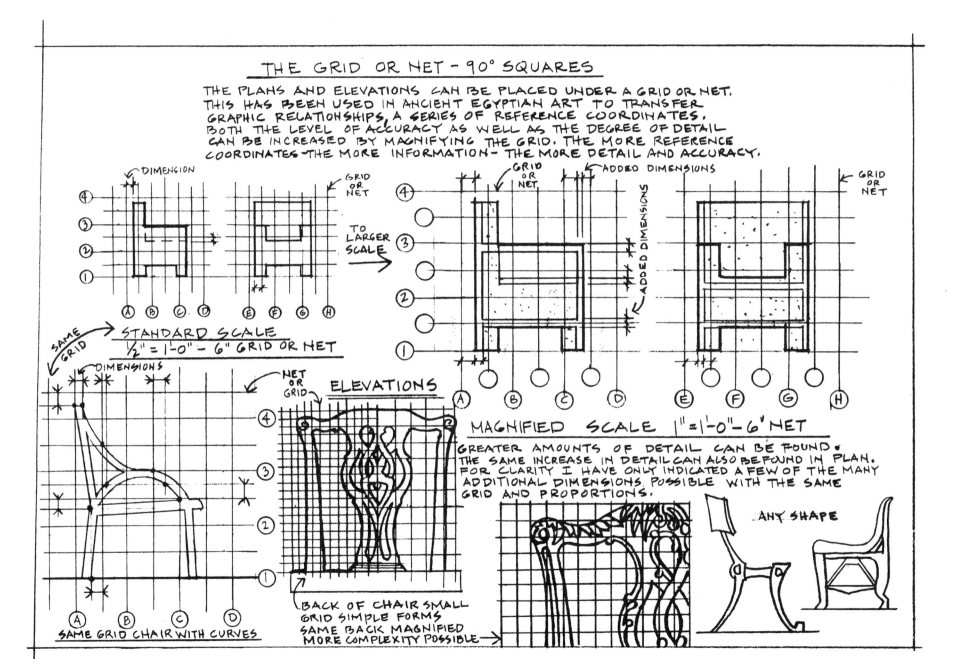

STANDARD SCALE
½" = 1'-0" - 6" GRID OR NET

ELEVATIONS

MAGNIFIED SCALE 1" = 1'-0" - 6" NET

GREATER AMOUNTS OF DETAIL CAN BE FOUND.
THE SAME INCREASE IN DETAIL CAN ALSO BE FOUND IN PLAN.
FOR CLARITY I HAVE ONLY INDICATED A FEW OF THE MANY
ADDITIONAL DIMENSIONS POSSIBLE WITH THE SAME
GRID AND PROPORTIONS.

ANY SHAPE

SAME GRID CHAIR WITH CURVES

BACK OF CHAIR SMALL
GRID SIMPLE FORMS
SAME BACK MAGNIFIED
MORE COMPLEXITY POSSIBLE →

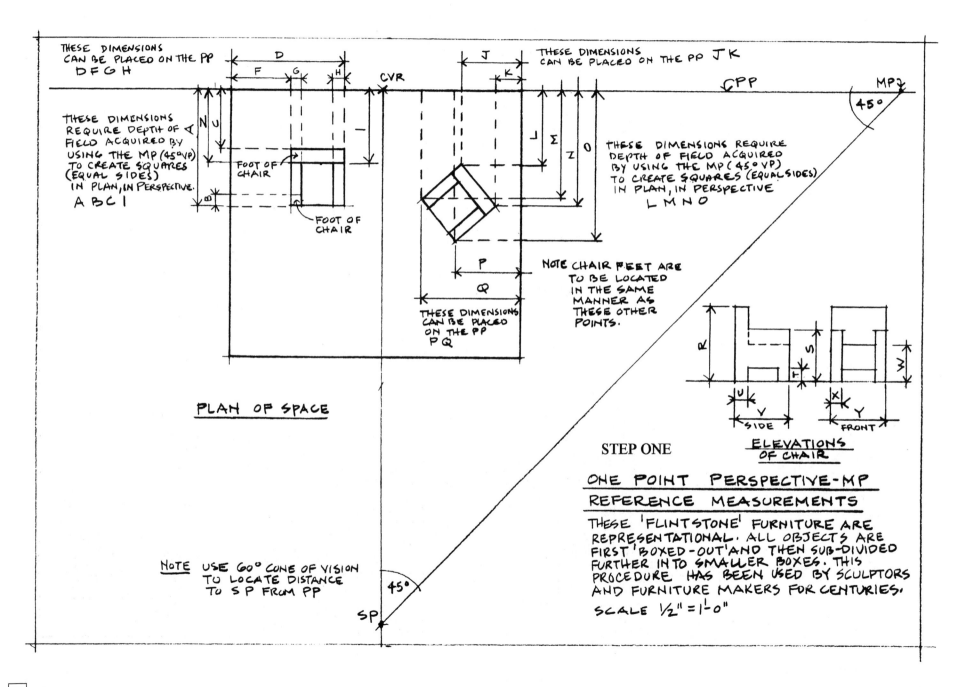

THESE DIMENSIONS CAN BE PLACED ON THE PP
DFGH

THESE DIMENSIONS CAN BE PLACED ON THE PP JK

CVR

PP

MP

45°

D

F G H

J

K

THESE DIMENSIONS REQUIRE DEPTH OF FIELD ACQUIRED BY USING THE MP (45°VP) TO CREATE SQUARES (EQUAL SIDES) IN PLAN, IN PERSPECTIVE.
A B C I

N U

FOOT OF CHAIR

FOOT OF CHAIR

THESE DIMENSIONS REQUIRE DEPTH OF FIELD ACQUIRED BY USING THE MP (45° VP) TO CREATE SQUARES (EQUAL SIDES) IN PLAN, IN PERSPECTIVE
L M N O

L Σ Z O

NOTE CHAIR FEET ARE TO BE LOCATED IN THE SAME MANNER AS THESE OTHER POINTS.

P

Q

THESE DIMENSIONS CAN BE PLACED ON THE PP
P Q

PLAN OF SPACE

NOTE USE 60° CONE OF VISION TO LOCATE DISTANCE TO SP FROM PP

45°

SP

R S T

U V

SIDE

W

X Y

FRONT

ELEVATIONS OF CHAIR

STEP ONE

ONE POINT PERSPECTIVE-MP

REFERENCE MEASUREMENTS

THESE 'FLINTSTONE' FURNITURE ARE REPRESENTATIONAL. ALL OBJECTS ARE FIRST 'BOXED-OUT' AND THEN SUB-DIVIDED FURTHER INTO SMALLER BOXES. THIS PROCEDURE HAS BEEN USED BY SCULPTORS AND FURNITURE MAKERS FOR CENTURIES.

SCALE ½" = 1'-0"

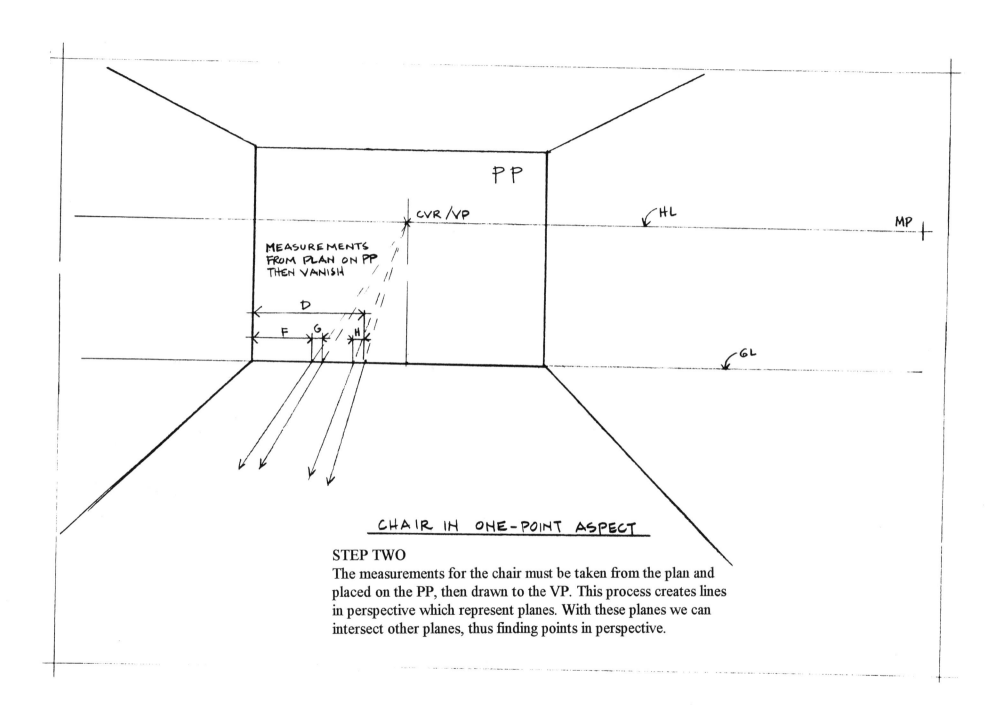

PP

CVR/VP

HL

MP

MEASUREMENTS
FROM PLAN ON PP
THEN VANISH

D

F G H

GL

CHAIR IN ONE-POINT ASPECT

STEP TWO

The measurements for the chair must be taken from the plan and
placed on the PP, then drawn to the VP. This process creates lines
in perspective which represent planes. With these planes we can
intersect other planes, thus finding points in perspective.

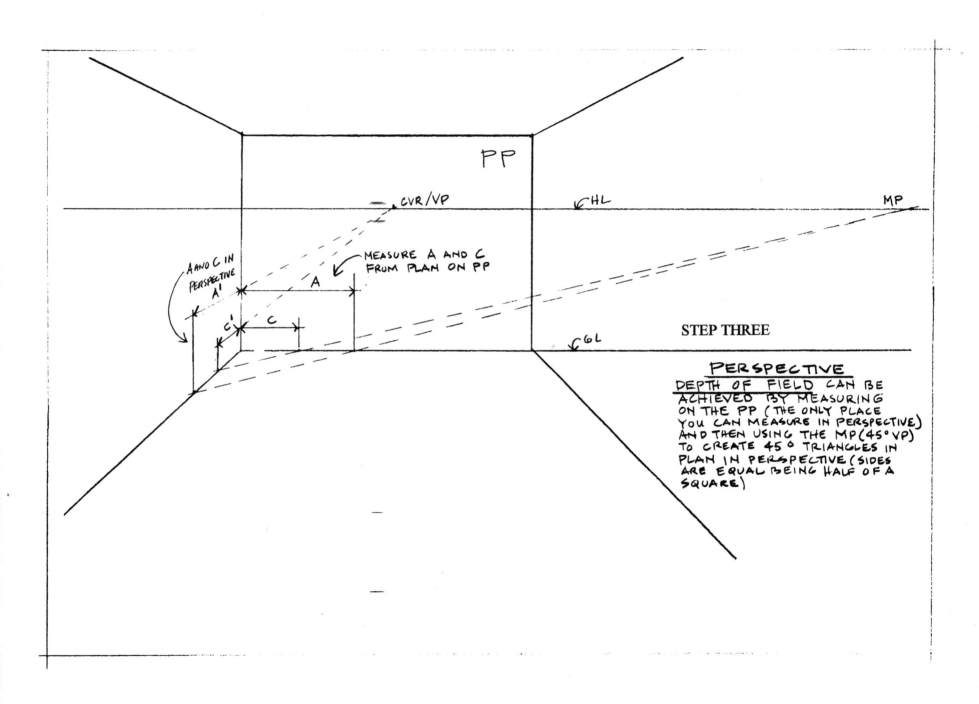

PP

CVR/VP — HL — MP

A AND C IN PERSPECTIVE
A'

MEASURE A AND C FROM PLAN ON PP

A

C'

C

STEP THREE

GL

PERSPECTIVE

DEPTH OF FIELD CAN BE ACHIEVED BY MEASURING ON THE PP (THE ONLY PLACE YOU CAN MEASURE IN PERSPECTIVE) AND THEN USING THE MP (45° VP) TO CREATE 45° TRIANGLES IN PLAN IN PERSPECTIVE (SIDES ARE EQUAL BEING HALF OF A SQUARE)

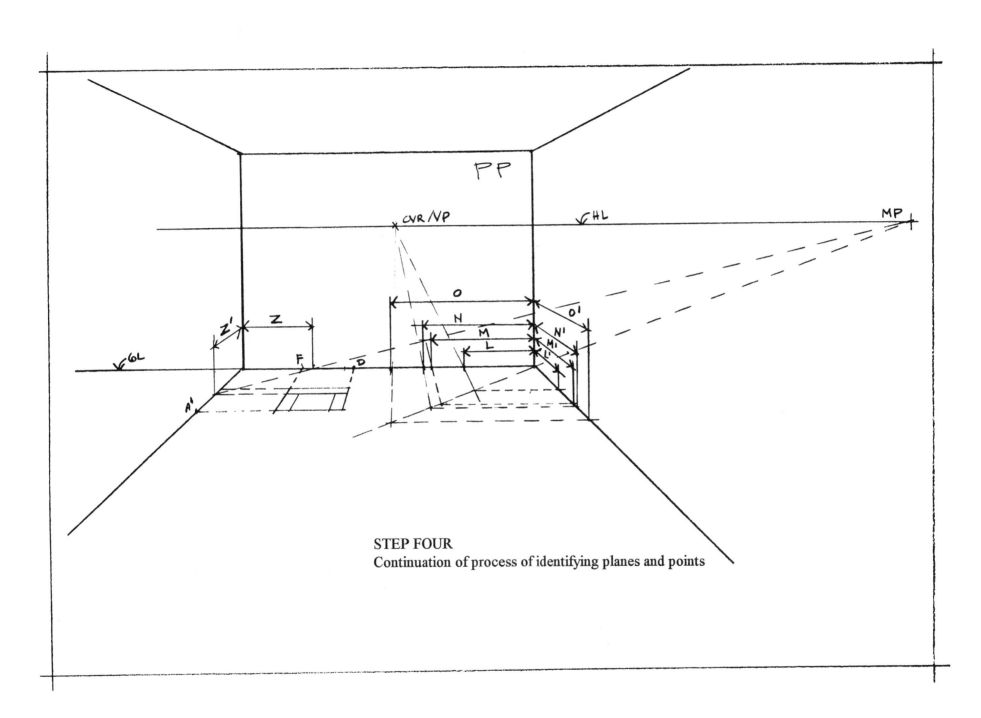

PP

CVR/VP   HL   MP

GL

Z'   Z   F   D

A'

O   O'

N   N'

M   M'

L   L'

STEP FOUR
Continuation of process of identifying planes and points

71

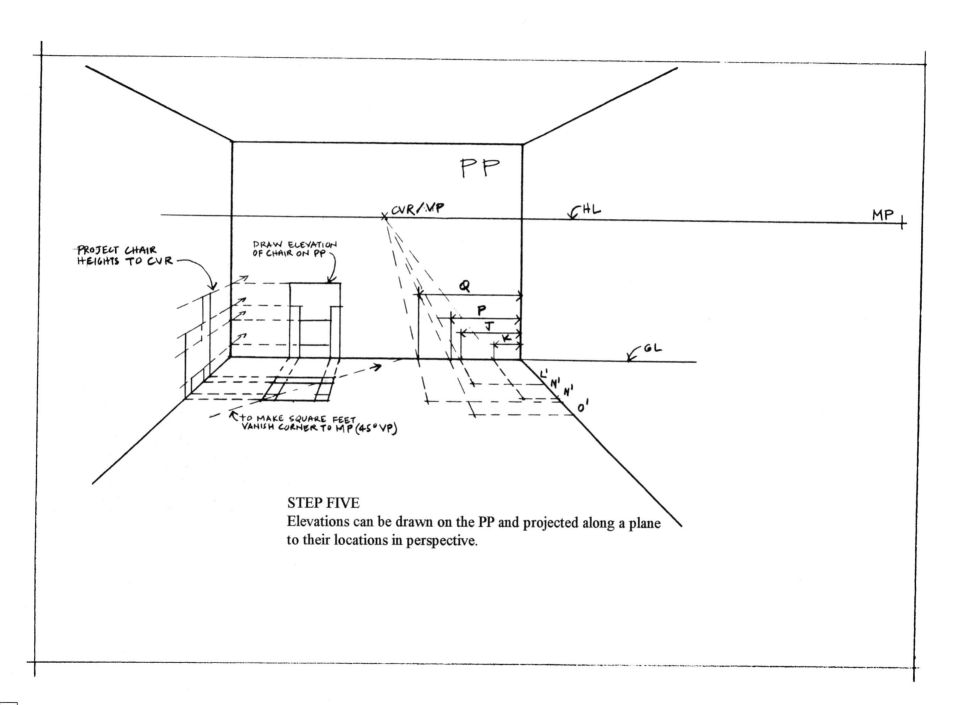

PP

CVR/VP   CHL   MP

PROJECT CHAIR
HEIGHTS TO CVR

DRAW ELEVATION
OF CHAIR ON PP

Q

P

J

K

GL

L¹ N¹ N¹ O¹

TO MAKE SQUARE FEET
VANISH CORNER TO MP (45° VP)

STEP FIVE
Elevations can be drawn on the PP and projected along a plane
to their locations in perspective.

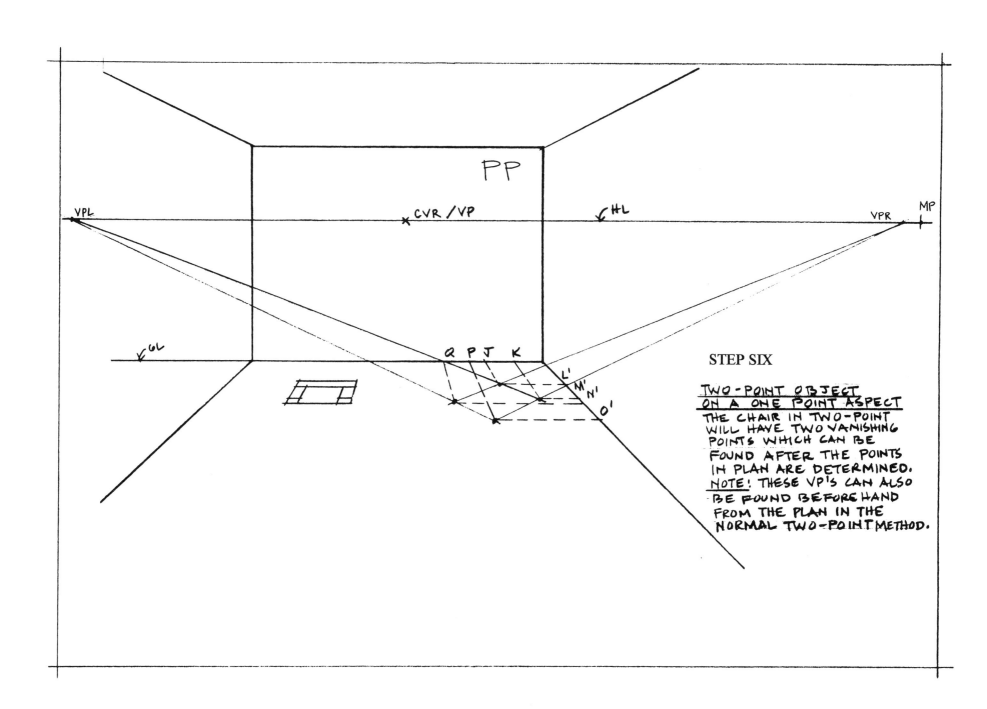

PP

VPL

CVR / VP   ⌐HL

VPR   MP

⌐GL

Q P J K

STEP SIX

L'
M'
N'
O'

<u>TWO-POINT OBJECT
ON A ONE POINT ASPECT</u>
THE CHAIR IN TWO-POINT
WILL HAVE TWO VANISHING
POINTS WHICH CAN BE
FOUND AFTER THE POINTS
IN PLAN ARE DETERMINED.
<u>NOTE!</u> THESE VP's CAN ALSO
BE FOUND BEFOREHAND
FROM THE PLAN IN THE
NORMAL TWO-POINT METHOD.

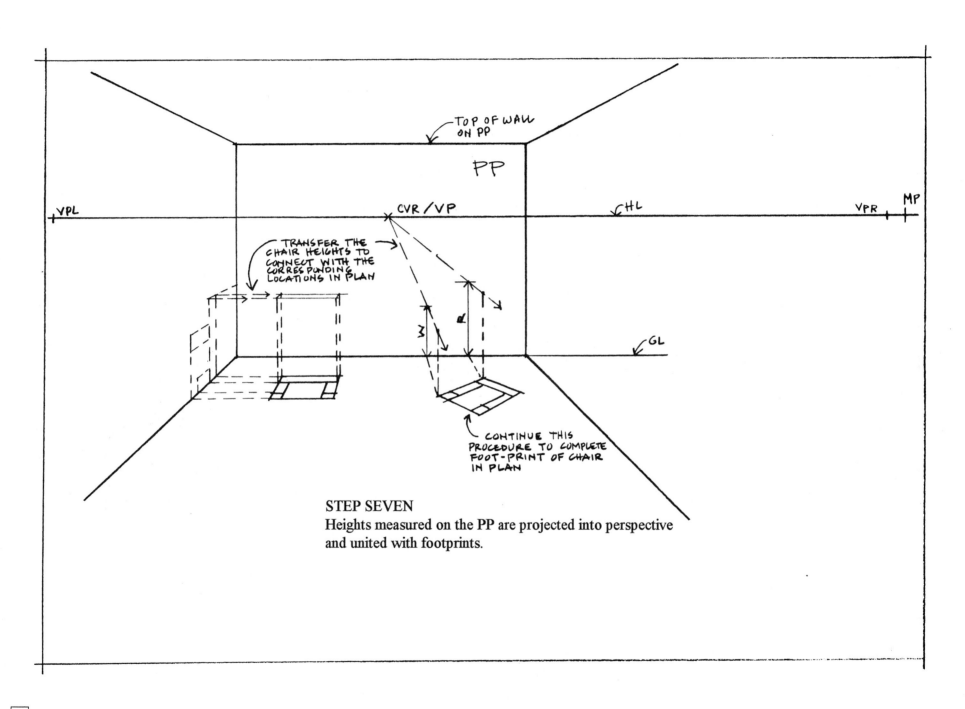

TOP OF WALL ON PP

PP

VPL

CVR/VP

HL

VPR

MP

TRANSFER THE CHAIR HEIGHTS TO CONNECT WITH THE CORRESPONDING LOCATIONS IN PLAN

GL

CONTINUE THIS PROCEDURE TO COMPLETE FOOT-PRINT OF CHAIR IN PLAN

STEP SEVEN
Heights measured on the PP are projected into perspective and united with footprints.

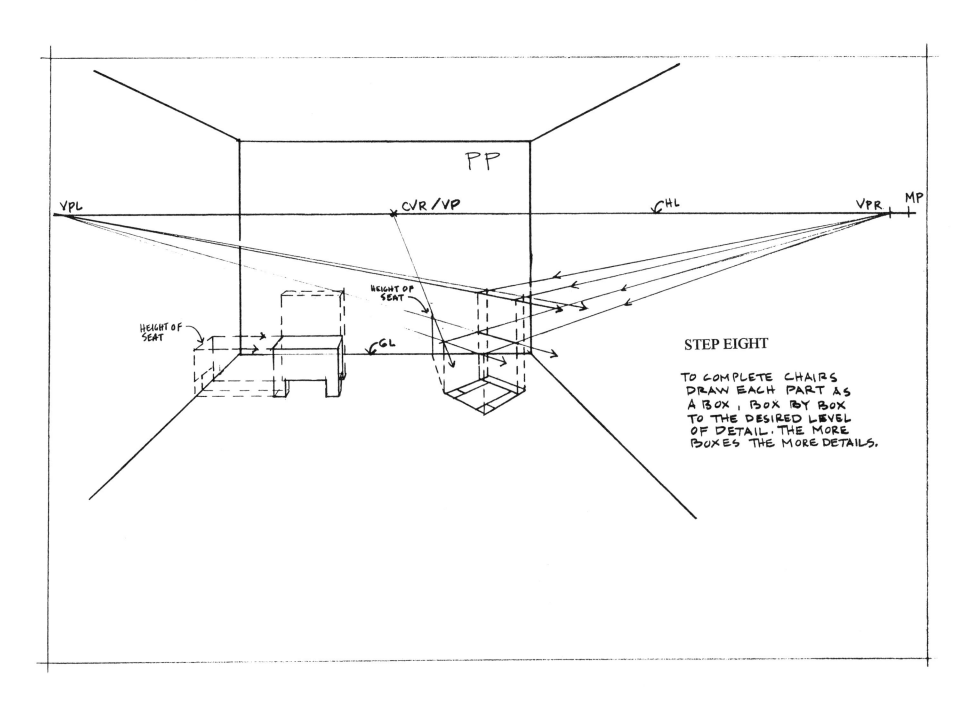

PP

VPL

CVR/VP

HL

VPR   MP

HEIGHT OF SEAT

HEIGHT OF SEAT

GL

STEP EIGHT

TO COMPLETE CHAIRS
DRAW EACH PART AS
A BOX, BOX BY BOX
TO THE DESIRED LEVEL
OF DETAIL. THE MORE
BOXES THE MORE DETAILS.

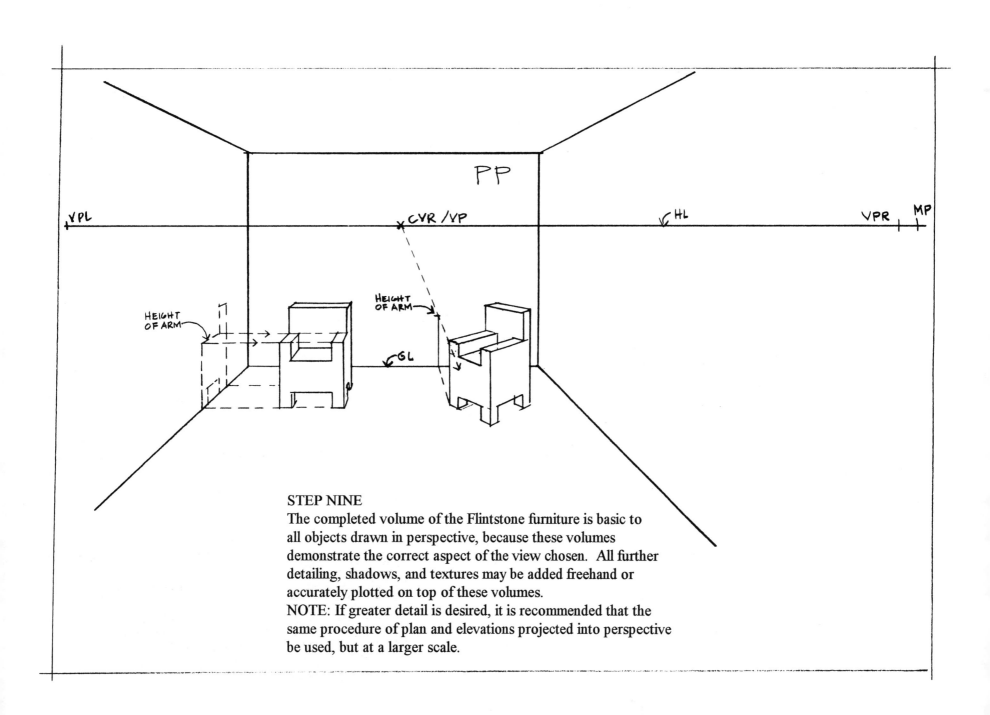

PP

YPL   CVR /VP   HL   VPR   MP

HEIGHT
OF ARM

HEIGHT
OF ARM

GL

STEP NINE
The completed volume of the Flintstone furniture is basic to
all objects drawn in perspective, because these volumes
demonstrate the correct aspect of the view chosen. All further
detailing, shadows, and textures may be added freehand or
accurately plotted on top of these volumes.
NOTE: If greater detail is desired, it is recommended that the
same procedure of plan and elevations projected into perspective
be used, but at a larger scale.

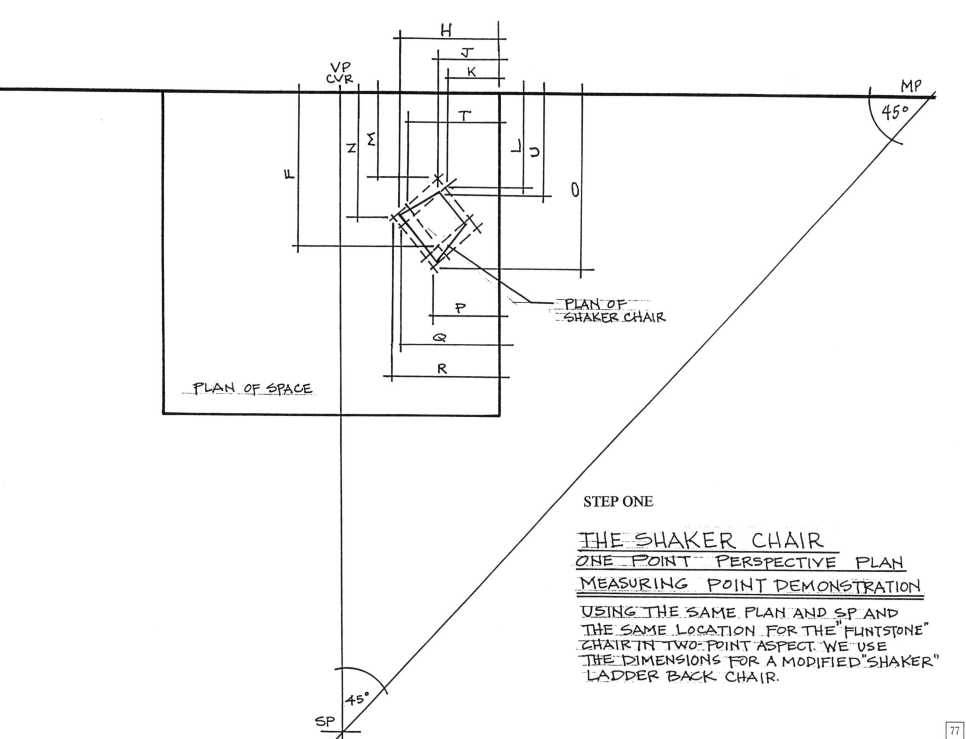

H

J

K

VP
CVR

MP

45°

T

N M

L U

F

O

PLAN OF
SHAKER CHAIR

P

Q

PLAN OF SPACE

R

STEP ONE

THE SHAKER CHAIR
ONE POINT PERSPECTIVE PLAN
MEASURING POINT DEMONSTRATION

USING THE SAME PLAN AND SP AND
THE SAME LOCATION FOR THE "FLINTSTONE"
CHAIR IN TWO-POINT ASPECT. WE USE
THE DIMENSIONS FOR A MODIFIED "SHAKER"
LADDER BACK CHAIR.

45°

SP

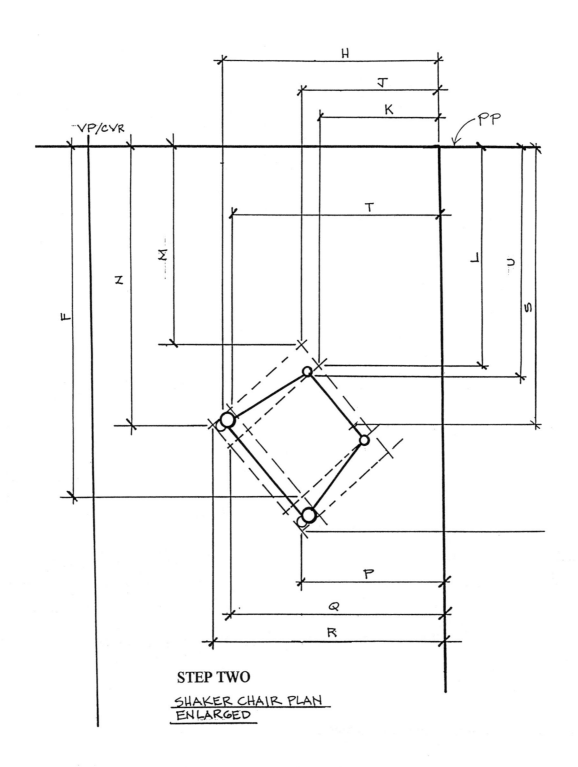

STEP TWO

SHAKER CHAIR PLAN
ENLARGED

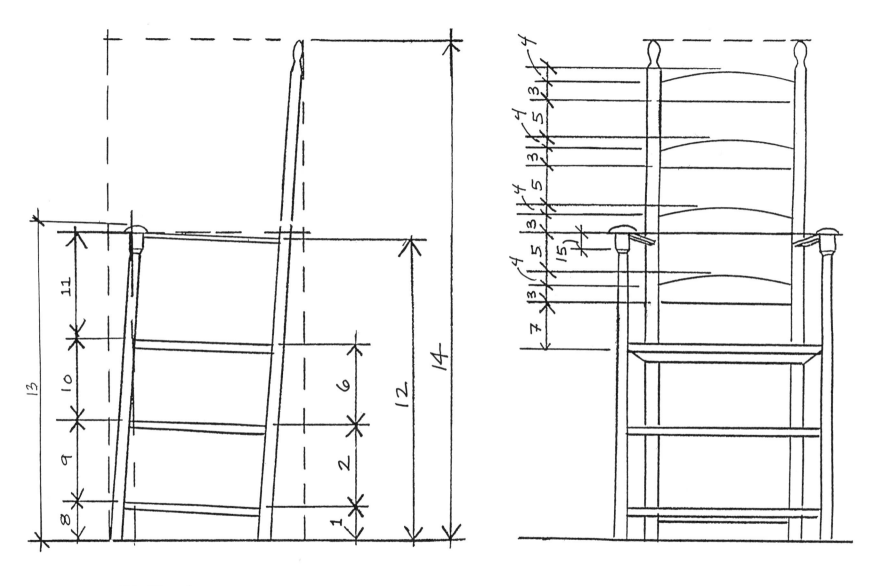

Side Elevation
Please note the incline of
the front and back legs.

ELEVATIONS OF SHAKER CHAIR   Front Elevation

The necessary dimensions are indicated by reference numbers.

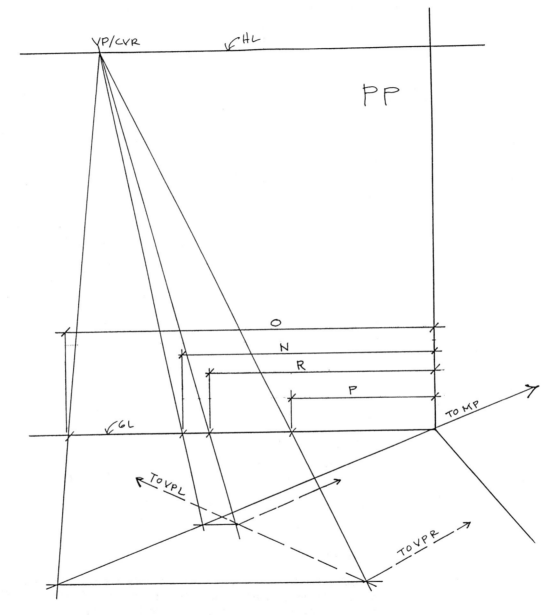

STEP THREE

FROM THE PLAN USING THE MP
LOCATE THE FOOTPRINT OF THE
CHAIR IN PERSPECTIVE

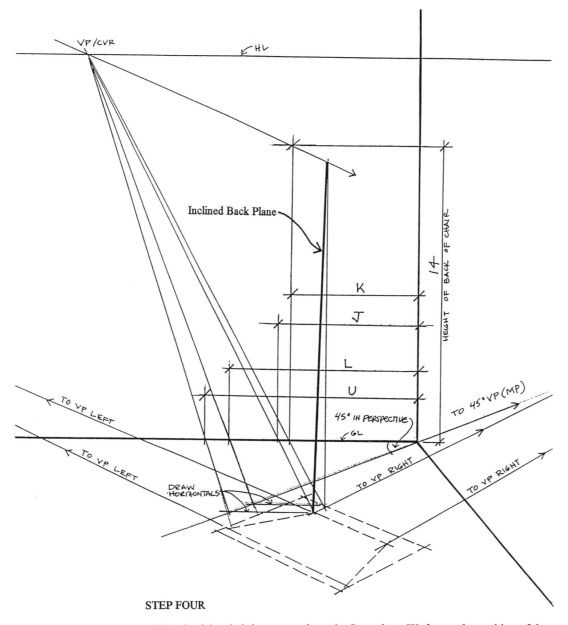

VP/CVR

HL

Inclined Back Plane

HEIGHT OF BACK OF CHAIR

14

K

J

L

U

TO 45° VP (MP)

TO VP LEFT

TO VP LEFT

45° IN PERSPECTIVE

GL

TO VP RIGHT

TO VP RIGHT

DRAW HORIZONTALS

STEP FOUR

The back of the chair is at an angle to the floor plane. We locate the position of the bottom in plan and the top height from the measurements on the PP. We next connect the points, top and bottom, and draw the inclined back plane. We can then transfer the measurements for the heights of the seat and other horizontals to the inclined back plane by using the VP.

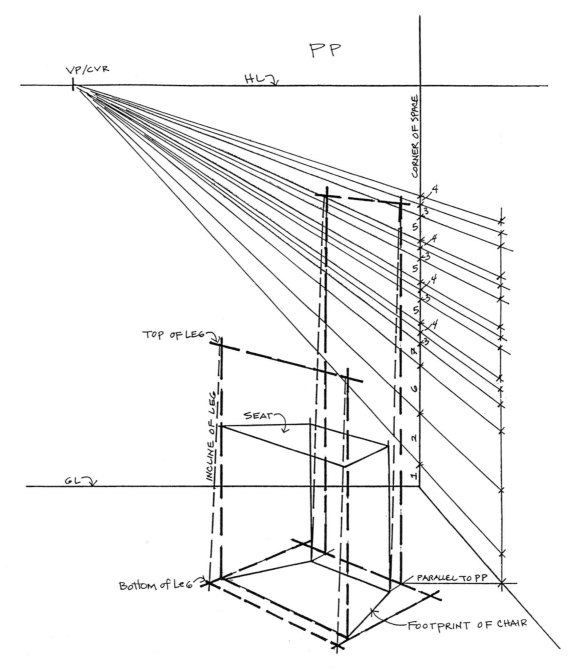

PP

VP/CVR

HL

CORNER OF SPACE

TOP OF LEG

INCLINE OF LEG

SEAT

GL

Bottom of LEG

PARALLEL TO PP

FOOTPRINT OF CHAIR

STEP FIVE

The front and back planes of the chair, as well as the seat,
are completed following the procedure described in Step Four.
Then add the heights (from the elevation) of the back slats on
the PP and project them forward from the VP into perspective.

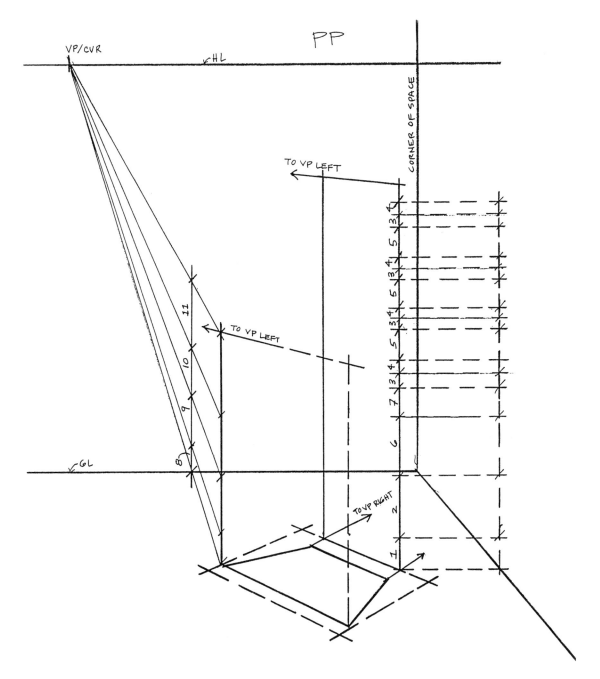

STEP SIX

The heights of the slats on the chair back are taken from their position in perspective and connected to their correct position over the footprint. Also, the heights of the seat and crossbar on the chair front are drawn on the PP and projected to their correct position over the footprint.

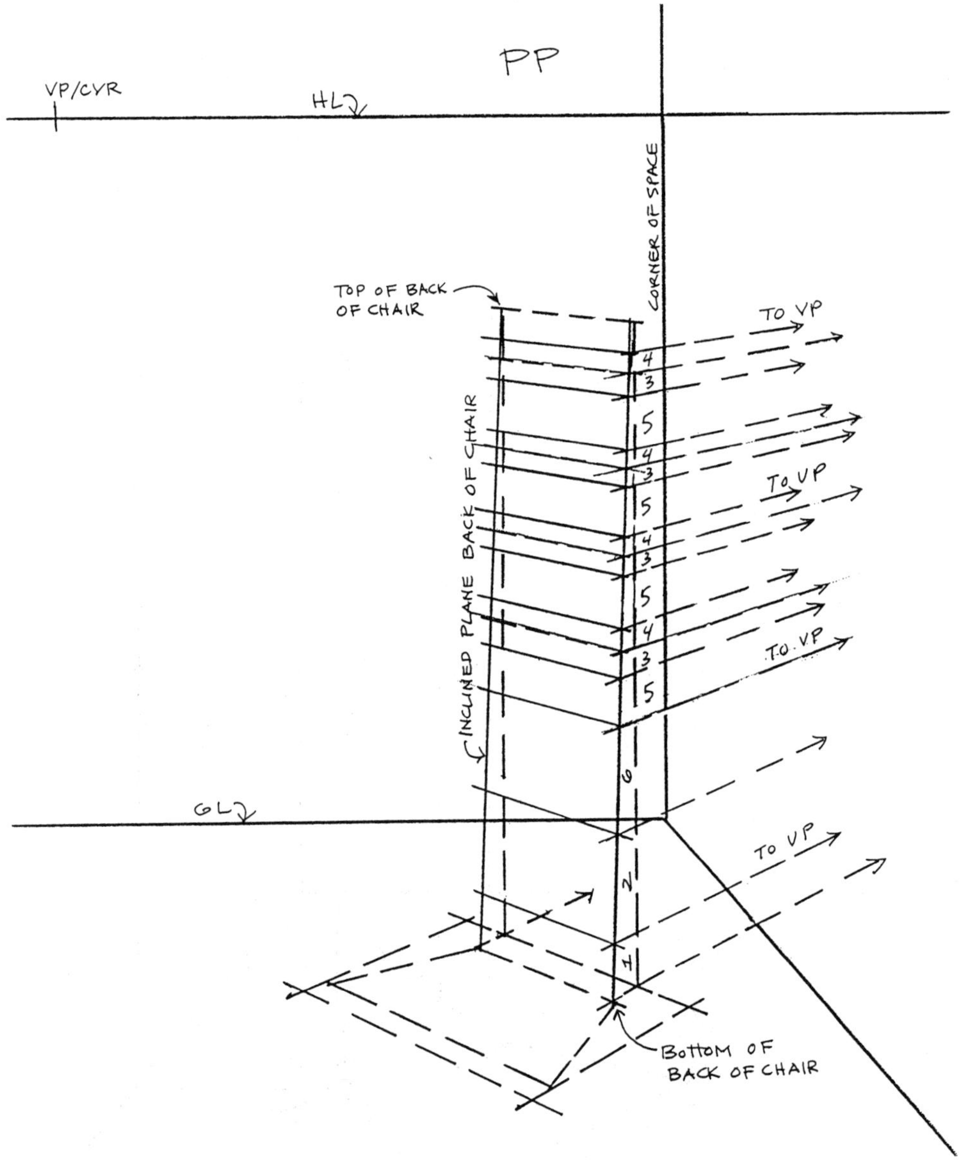

PP

VP/CVR HL↲

CORNER OF SPACE

TOP OF BACK OF CHAIR

INCLINED PLANE BACK OF CHAIR

TO VP

4
3
5
4
3
5
4
3
5
4
3
5

TO VP

TO VP

TO VP

GL↲

TO VP

BOTTOM OF BACK OF CHAIR

STEP SEVEN

THE BACK OF THE CHAIR
IS AT AN ANGLE. WE LOCATE
THE POSITION OF THE BOTTOM
IN PLAN AND THE TOP HEIGHT
FROM THE PICTURE PLANE.
WE CONNECT THE POINTS AND
THEN TRANSFER THE 3, 4, 5
MEASUREMENTS TO THE
NEW INCLINED BACK OF THE
CHAIR.

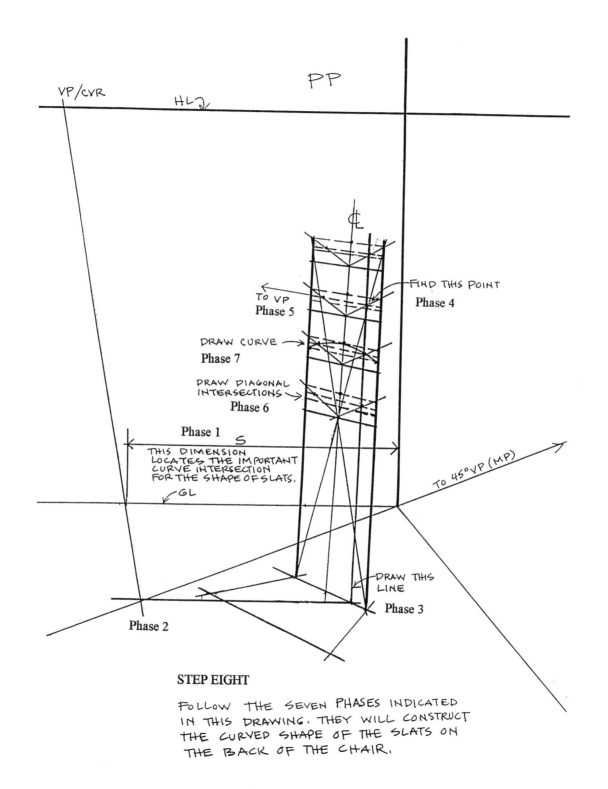

PP

VP/CVR

HL

⌀

FIND THIS POINT
Phase 4

TO VP
Phase 5

DRAW CURVE
Phase 7

DRAW DIAGONAL
INTERSECTIONS
Phase 6

Phase 1

S

THIS DIMENSION
LOCATES THE IMPORTANT
CURVE INTERSECTION
FOR THE SHAPE OF SLATS.

GL

TO 45° VP (MP)

DRAW THIS
LINE
Phase 3

Phase 2

STEP EIGHT

FOLLOW THE SEVEN PHASES INDICATED
IN THIS DRAWING. THEY WILL CONSTRUCT
THE CURVED SHAPE OF THE SLATS ON
THE BACK OF THE CHAIR.

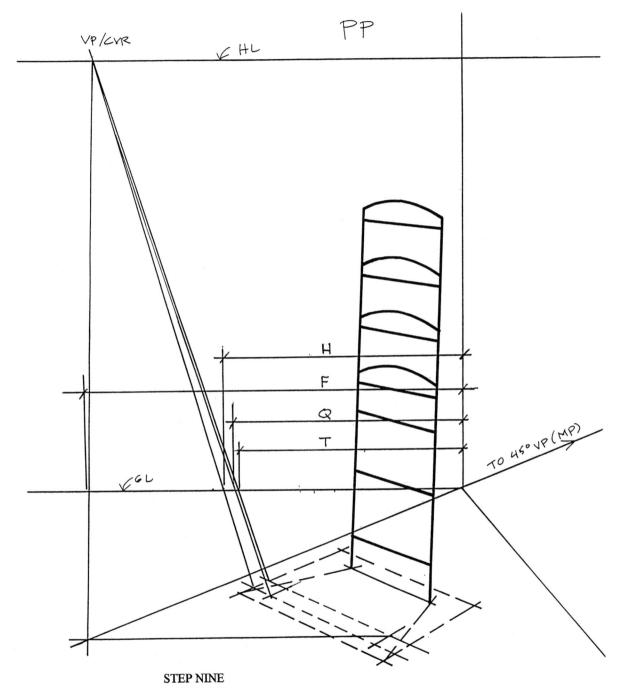

VP/CVR

PP

HL

H
F
Q
T

TO 45° VP (MP)

GL

STEP NINE

FROM THE PLAN LOCATE THE POSITIONS
OF THE FRONT LEGS OF THE CHAIR
WE ARE FIRST MAKING BOXES.

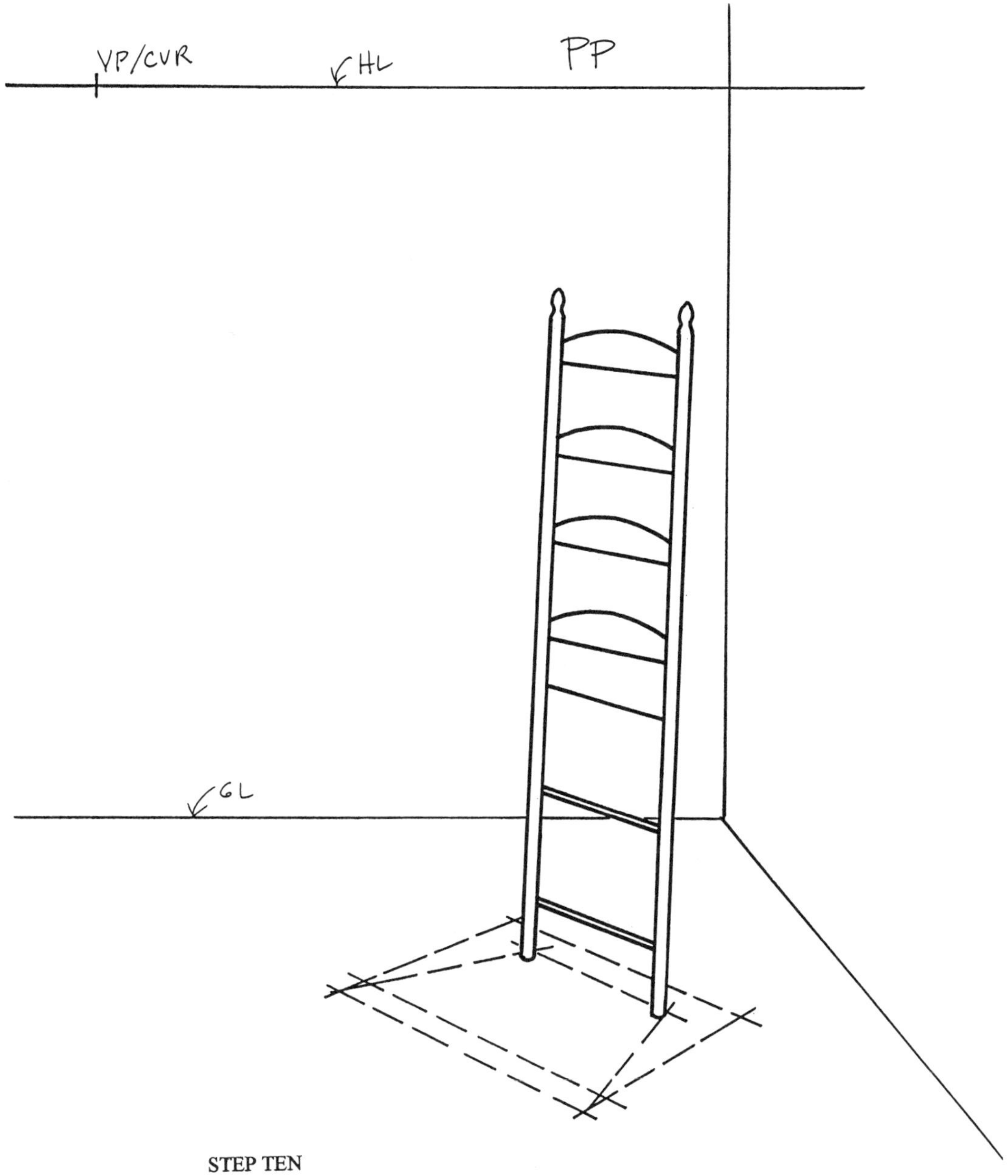

VP/CVR   ↙HL   PP

↙GL

STEP TEN

WE CAN COMPLETE THE LADDER-BACK
BY RETURNING TO THE PLAN AND ADDING
THE THICKNESS OF THE TWO LEGS. THE ROUND
SHAPE IN THE PLAN MAY BE PLOTTED WITHIN
THE EXISTING CORNER OF THE PLAN IN PERSPECTIVE
AND SIMPLY DRAWN FOLLOWING THE ANGLE
OF THE INCLINE OF THE BACK.

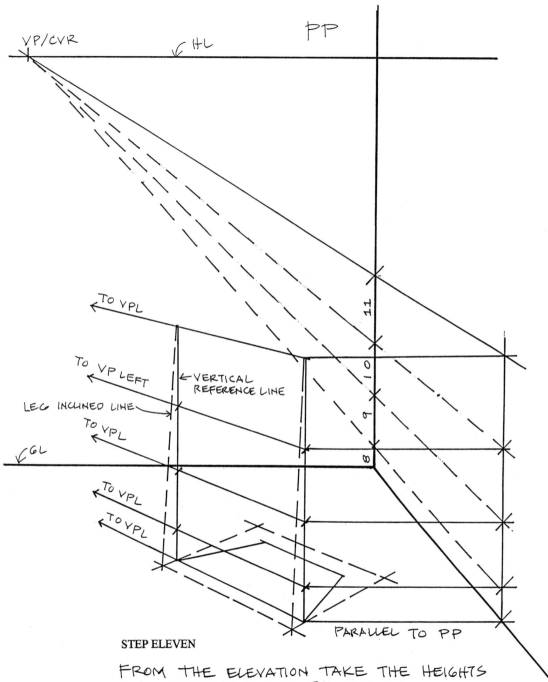

VP/CVR

PP

HL

TO VPL

TO VP LEFT

← VERTICAL REFERENCE LINE

LEG INCLINED LINE →

TO VPL

GL

TO VPL

TO VPL

11

10

9

8

PARALLEL TO PP

STEP ELEVEN

FROM THE ELEVATION TAKE THE HEIGHTS
AND PLACE THEM ON THE PP AND
PROJECT THEM FORWARD INTO THE
PERSPECTIVE ON THE VERTICAL REFERENCE LINE.

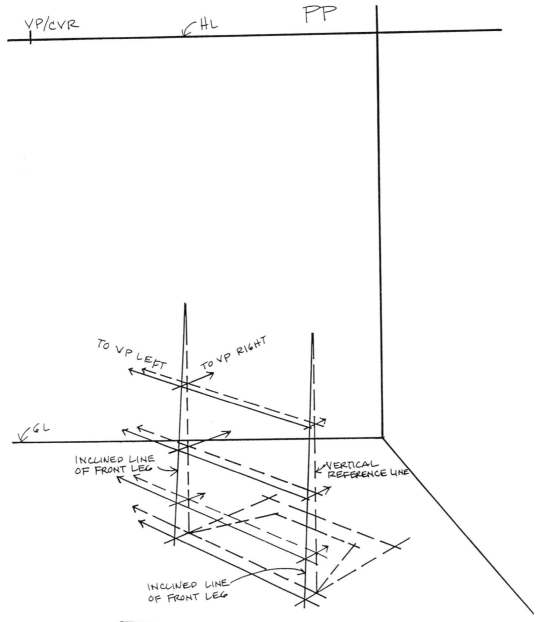

VP/CVR

HL

PP

TO VP LEFT

TO VP RIGHT

GL

INCLINED LINE
OF FRONT LEG

VERTICAL
REFERENCE LINE

INCLINED LINE
OF FRONT LEG

STEP TWELVE

FROM THE VERTICAL REFERENCE LINE
USING THE VP'S RIGHT AND LEFT TRANSFER
THE HEIGHTS TO THE INCLINED LINE OF
THE FRONT PLANE OF THE FRONT CHAIR LEGS.

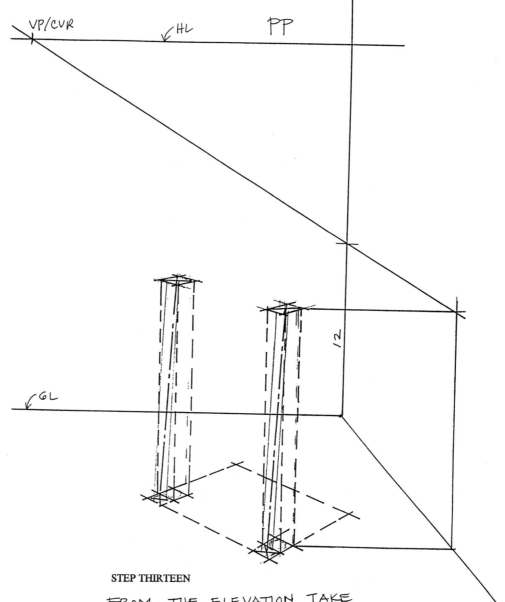

VP/CVR   HL   PP

12

GL

STEP THIRTEEN

FROM THE ELEVATION TAKE
THE HEIGHT OF THE FRONT LEGS
AND PLACE IT ON THE PP.
PROJECT FORWARD FROM THE PP
AND INTO PERSPECTIVE. THEN BOX-IN
THE OVER-ALL VOLUME OF THE FRONT-LEGS.
BE SURE TO LOCATE THE CENTERS
WITH DIAGONALS. CONNECT THE
CENTERS AND YOU HAVE THE CENTER
LINES OF THE INCLINED LEGS.

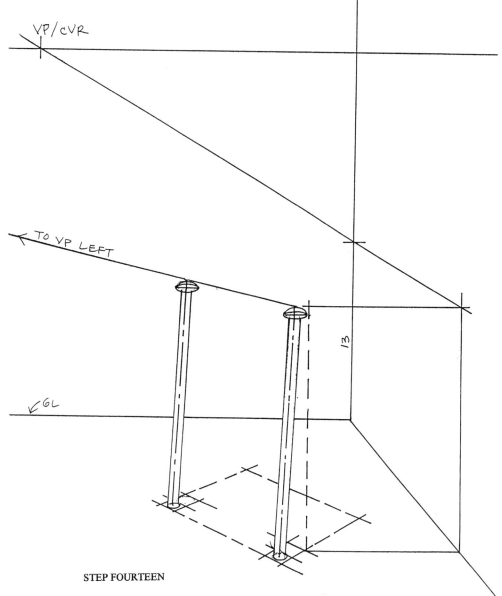

VP/CVR

TO VP LEFT

GL

13

STEP FOURTEEN

THE COMPLETED SHAPE OF THE
FRONT LEGS MAY BE DRAWN BY
FIRST DRAWING IN PLAN IN PERSPECTIVE
THE CIRCLE OF THE FOOT OF THE LEG,
AND THE CIRCLE AT THE TOP USING THE
BOX AND CENTERS ALREADY EXISTING.
CONNECT THE TOP AND BOTTOM CIRCLE
AND ADD THE CAP.

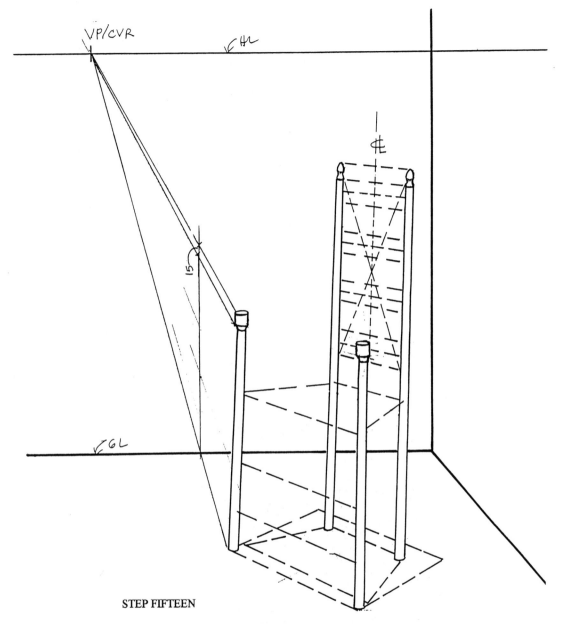

STEP FIFTEEN

FROM THE ELEVATION FURTHER DETAILS
MAY BE PROJECTED FROM THE PP INTO
THE EXISTING PERSPECTIVE. THE CHAIR
MAY BE ASSEMBLED. PLEASE NOTE:
(EACH STEP SHOULD BE DRAWN ON A SEPARATE
PIECE OF WHITE TRACE AND AT THIS POINT
THEY SHOULD BE TRACED TOGETHER)

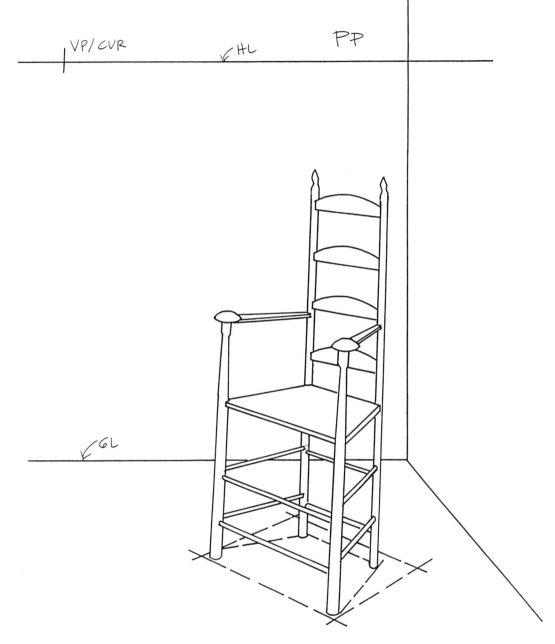

VP/CVR

HL

PP

GL

STEP SIXTEEN

FURTHER DETAILS, CHARACTER, AND SHADING
MAY BE ADDED.

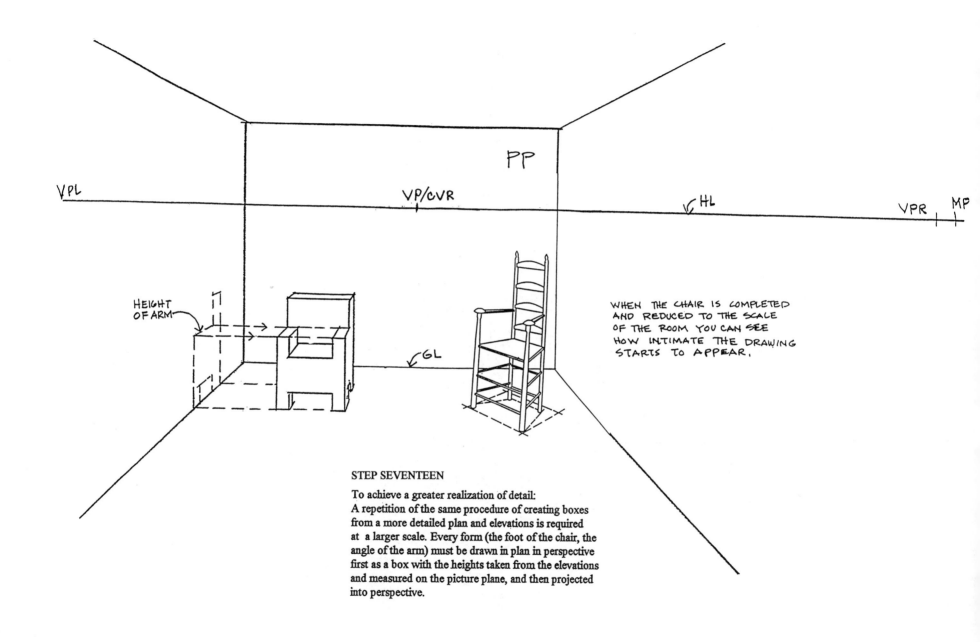

PP

VPL

VP/CVR

HL

VPR

MP

HEIGHT OF ARM

GL

WHEN THE CHAIR IS COMPLETED AND REDUCED TO THE SCALE OF THE ROOM YOU CAN SEE HOW INTIMATE THE DRAWING STARTS TO APPEAR.

STEP SEVENTEEN

To achieve a greater realization of detail:
A repetition of the same procedure of creating boxes from a more detailed plan and elevations is required at a larger scale. Every form (the foot of the chair, the angle of the arm) must be drawn in plan in perspective first as a box with the heights taken from the elevations and measured on the picture plane, and then projected into perspective.

NOTES

STAIRS/SPIRAL STAIRS

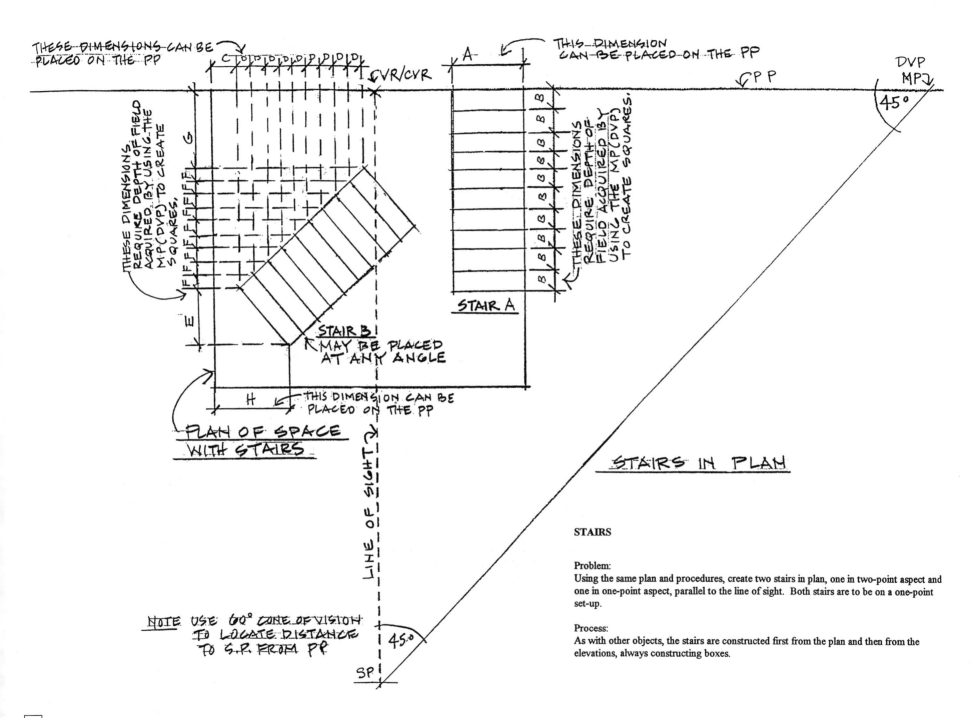

THESE DIMENSIONS CAN BE PLACED ON THE PP

THIS DIMENSION CAN BE PLACED ON THE PP

DVP MP

CVR/CVR

PP

45°

THESE DIMENSIONS REQUIRE DEPTH OF FIELD ACQUIRED BY USING THE MP(DVP) TO CREATE SQUARES.

THESE DIMENSIONS REQUIRE DEPTH OF FIELD ACQUIRED BY USING THE MP(DVP) TO CREATE SQUARES.

STAIR A

STAIR B MAY BE PLACED AT ANY ANGLE

THIS DIMENSION CAN BE PLACED ON THE PP

PLAN OF SPACE WITH STAIRS

LINE OF SIGHT

STAIRS IN PLAN

NOTE USE 60° CONE OF VISION TO LOCATE DISTANCE TO S.P. FROM PP

45°

SP

STAIRS

Problem:
Using the same plan and procedures, create two stairs in plan, one in two-point aspect and one in one-point aspect, parallel to the line of sight. Both stairs are to be on a one-point set-up.

Process:
As with other objects, the stairs are constructed first from the plan and then from the elevations, always constructing boxes.

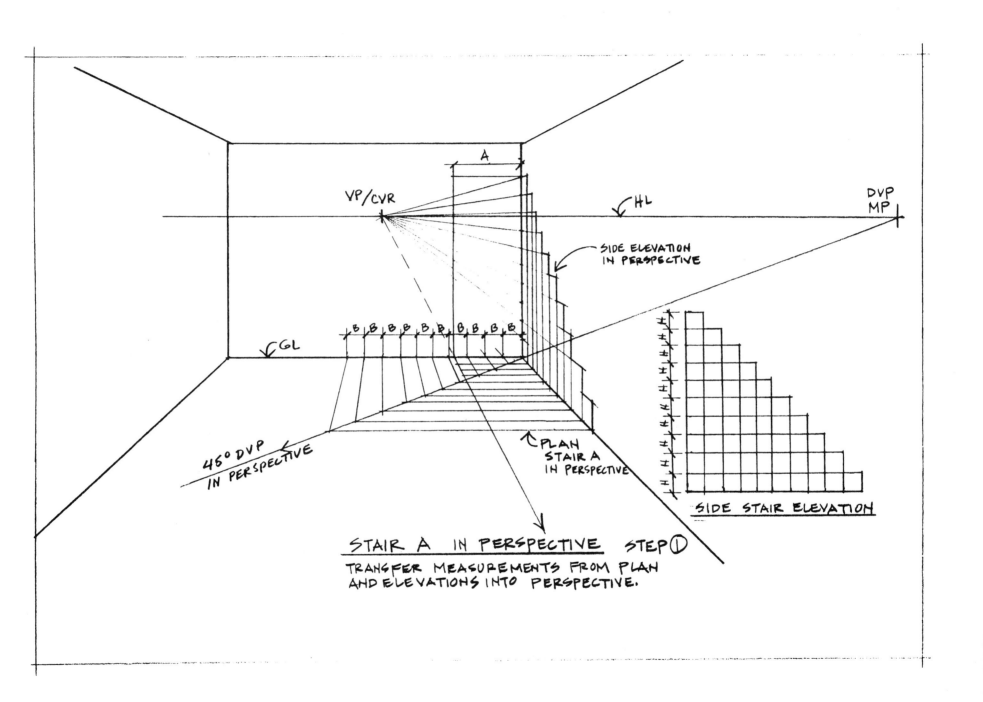

VP/CVR

HL

DVP MP

A

SIDE ELEVATION IN PERSPECTIVE

GL

B B B B B B B B B B

450 DVP IN PERSPECTIVE

PLAN STAIR A IN PERSPECTIVE

SIDE STAIR ELEVATION

STAIR A IN PERSPECTIVE STEP ①
TRANSFER MEASUREMENTS FROM PLAN
AND ELEVATIONS INTO PERSPECTIVE.

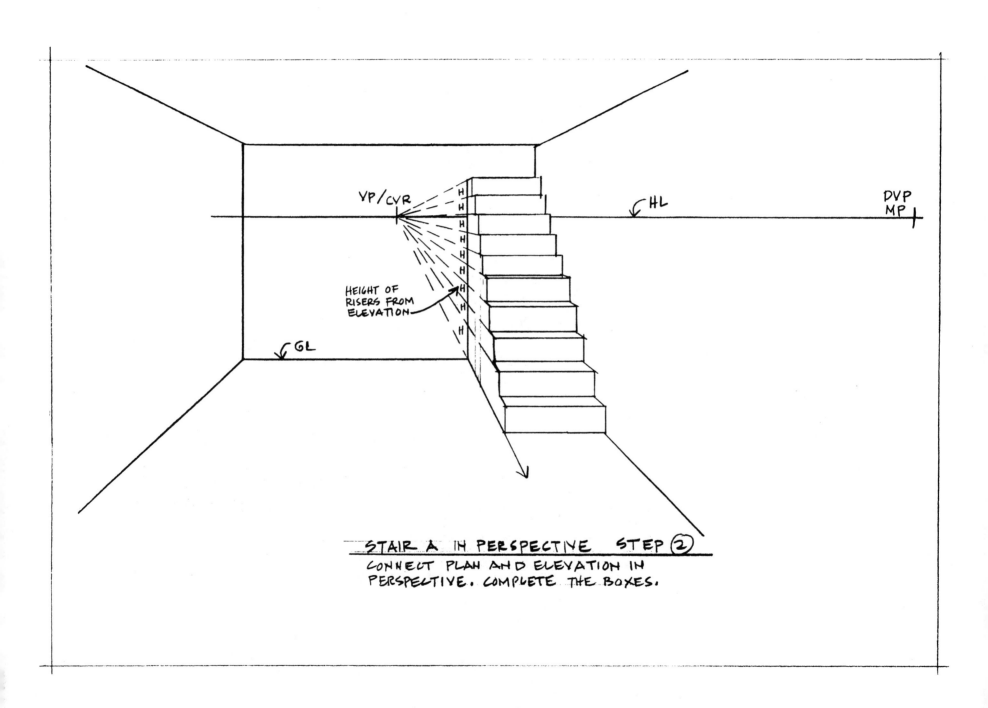

VP/CVR

DVP
MP

HL

HEIGHT OF
RISERS FROM
ELEVATION

GL

H
H
H
H
H
H
H
H
H
H

STAIR A IN PERSPECTIVE   STEP ②
CONNECT PLAN AND ELEVATION IN
PERSPECTIVE. COMPLETE THE BOXES.

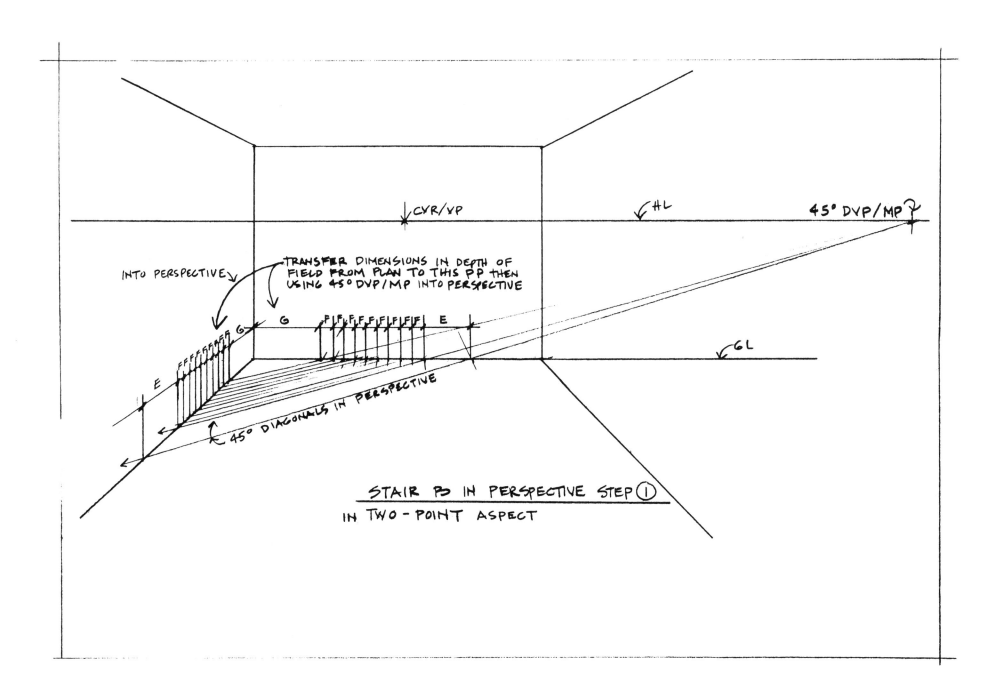

CYR/VP

↙ HL

45° DVP/MP ↙

INTO PERSPECTIVE ↙

↗ TRANSFER DIMENSIONS IN DEPTH OF
FIELD FROM PLAN TO THIS PP THEN
USING 45° DVP/MP INTO PERSPECTIVE

G   G   F|F|F|F|F|F|F|F|F|F| E

E   FFFFFFFFF   G

GL

↙ 45° DIAGONALS IN PERSPECTIVE

E

STAIR P3 IN PERSPECTIVE STEP ①
IN TWO-POINT ASPECT

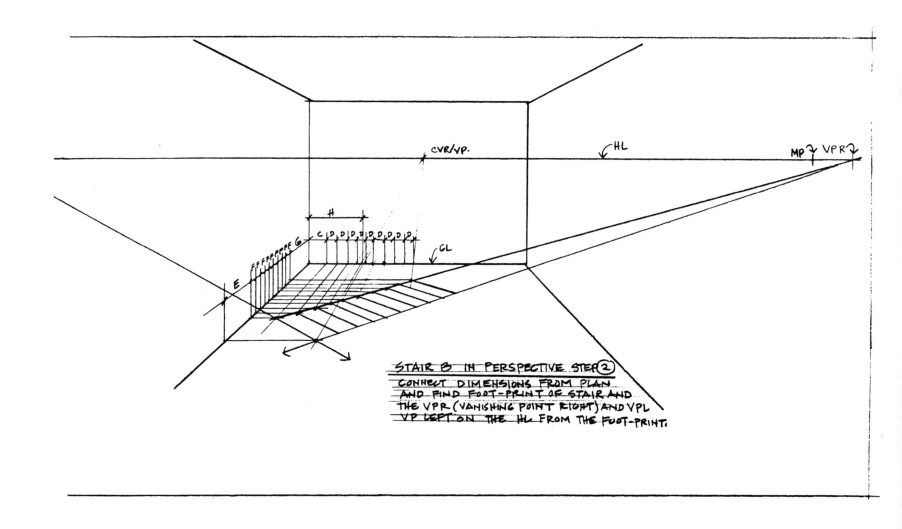

STAIR B IN PERSPECTIVE STEP ②
CONNECT DIMENSIONS FROM PLAN
AND FIND FOOT-PRINT OF STAIR AND
THE VPR (VANISHING POINT RIGHT) AND VPL
VP LEFT ON THE HL FROM THE FOOT-PRINT.

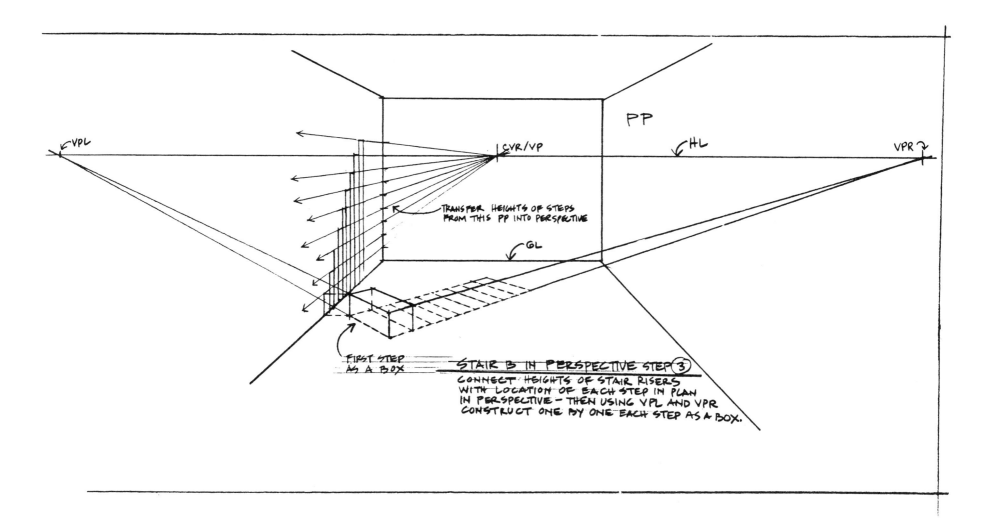

VPL

PP

CVR/VP

HL

VPR

TRANSFER HEIGHTS OF STEPS
FROM THIS PP INTO PERSPECTIVE

GL

FIRST STEP
AS A BOX

STAIR B IN PERSPECTIVE STEP ③

CONNECT HEIGHTS OF STAIR RISERS
WITH LOCATION OF EACH STEP IN PLAN
IN PERSPECTIVE - THEN USING VPL AND VPR
CONSTRUCT ONE BY ONE EACH STEP AS A BOX.

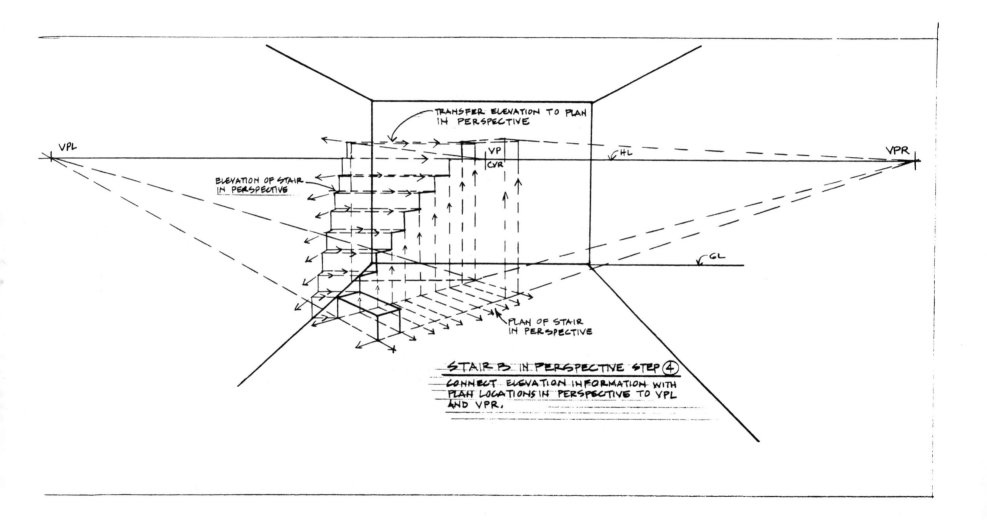

TRANSFER ELEVATION TO PLAN
IN PERSPECTIVE

VPL

VP
CVR

HL

VPR

ELEVATION OF STAIR
IN PERSPECTIVE

GL

PLAN OF STAIR
IN PERSPECTIVE

STAIR B IN PERSPECTIVE STEP ④

CONNECT ELEVATION INFORMATION WITH
PLAN LOCATIONS IN PERSPECTIVE TO VPL
AND VPR.

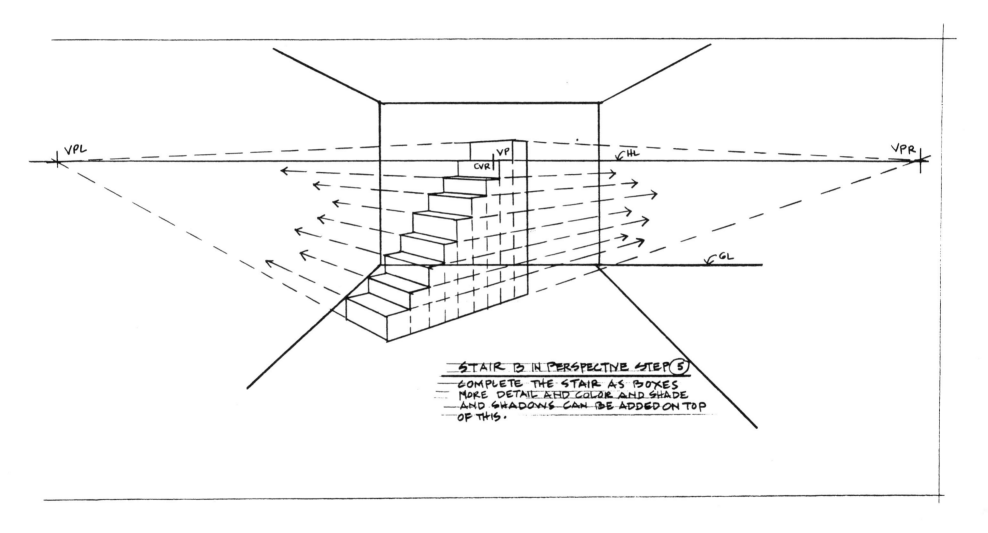

VPL

VPR

VP

CVR

HL

GL

STAIR B IN PERSPECTIVE STEP ⑤
COMPLETE THE STAIR AS BOXES
MORE DETAIL AND COLOR AND SHADE
AND SHADOWS CAN BE ADDED ON TOP
OF THIS.

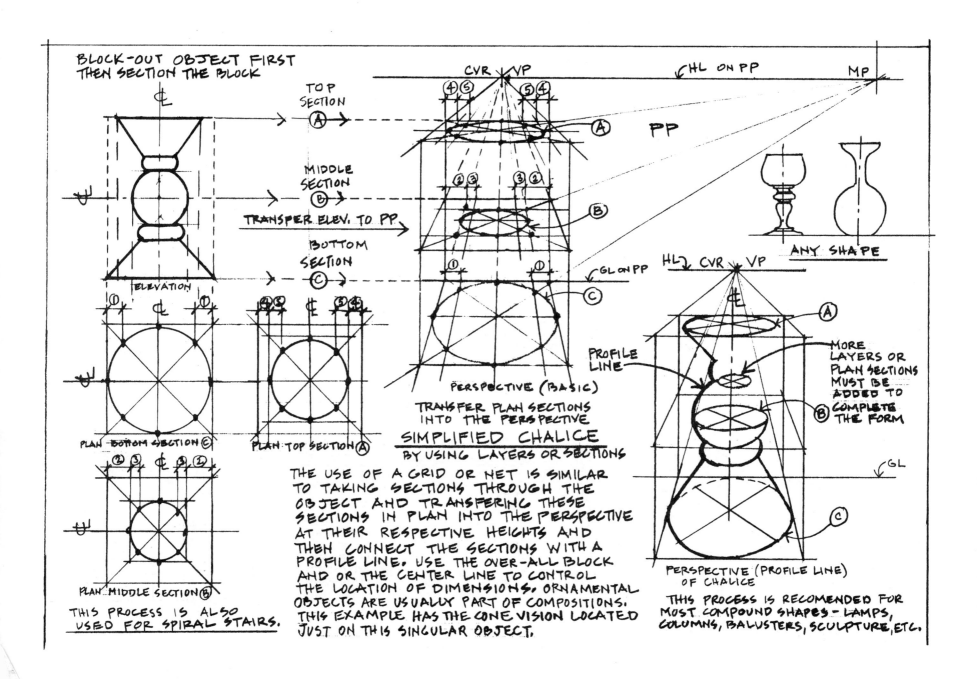

BLOCK-OUT OBJECT FIRST
THEN SECTION THE BLOCK

TOP
SECTION
(A)

MIDDLE
SECTION
(B)

TRANSFER ELEV. TO P.P.

BOTTOM
SECTION
(C)

ELEVATION

PLAN BOTTOM SECTION (C)

PLAN TOP SECTION (A)

PLAN MIDDLE SECTION (B)

THIS PROCESS IS ALSO
USED FOR SPIRAL STAIRS.

CVR   VP   CHL ON PP   MP

PP

(A)

(B)

GL ON PP

(C)

PERSPECTIVE (BASIC)

TRANSFER PLAN SECTIONS
INTO THE PERSPECTIVE

SIMPLIFIED CHALICE
BY USING LAYERS OR SECTIONS

THE USE OF A GRID OR NET IS SIMILAR
TO TAKING SECTIONS THROUGH THE
OBJECT AND TRANSFERING THESE
SECTIONS IN PLAN INTO THE PERSPECTIVE
AT THEIR RESPECTIVE HEIGHTS AND
THEN CONNECT THE SECTIONS WITH A
PROFILE LINE. USE THE OVER-ALL BLOCK
AND OR THE CENTER LINE TO CONTROL
THE LOCATION OF DIMENSIONS. ORNAMENTAL
OBJECTS ARE USUALLY PART OF COMPOSITIONS.
THIS EXAMPLE HAS THE CONE VISION LOCATED
JUST ON THIS SINGULAR OBJECT.

ANY SHAPE

HL   CVR   VP

(A)

PROFILE
LINE

MORE
LAYERS OR
PLAN SECTIONS
MUST BE
ADDED TO
(B) COMPLETE
THE FORM

GL

(C)

PERSPECTIVE (PROFILE LINE)
OF CHALICE

THIS PROCESS IS RECOMENDED FOR
MOST COMPOUND SHAPES - LAMPS,
COLUMNS, BALUSTERS, SCULPTURE, ETC.

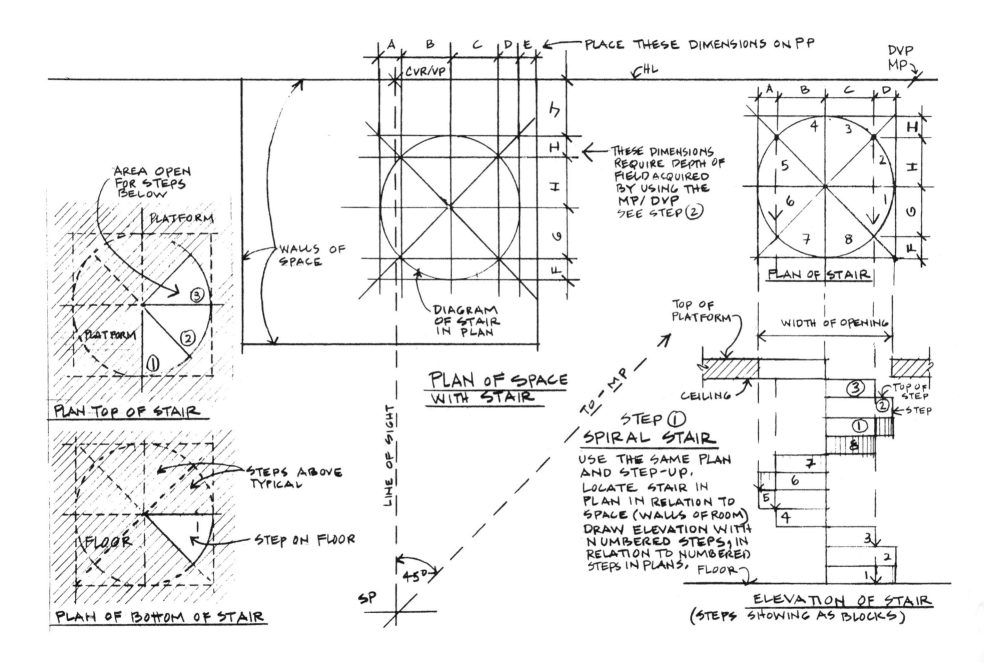

AREA OPEN
FOR STEPS
BELOW

PLATFORM

③

PLATFORM

②

①

PLAN TOP OF STAIR

STEPS ABOVE
TYPICAL

FLOOR

STEP ON FLOOR

PLAN OF BOTTOM OF STAIR

A B C D E ← PLACE THESE DIMENSIONS ON PP

CVR/VP

HL

THESE DIMENSIONS
REQUIRE DEPTH OF
FIELD ACQUIRED
BY USING THE
MP/DVP
SEE STEP ②

WALLS OF
SPACE

DIAGRAM
OF STAIR
IN PLAN

PLAN OF SPACE
WITH STAIR

LINE OF SIGHT

45°

SP

TO MP

DVP
MP

A B C D

4 3

5 2

6 1

7 8

PLAN OF STAIR

H
I
G
F

TOP OF
PLATFORM

WIDTH OF OPENING

CEILING

③
②

TOP OF
STEP

STEP

①

7

6

5

4

STEP ①
SPIRAL STAIR

USE THE SAME PLAN
AND STEP-UP.
LOCATE STAIR IN
PLAN IN RELATION TO
SPACE (WALLS OF ROOM)
DRAW ELEVATION WITH
NUMBERED STEPS, IN
RELATION TO NUMBERED
STEPS IN PLANS. FLOOR

3

2

1

ELEVATION OF STAIR
(STEPS SHOWING AS BLOCKS)

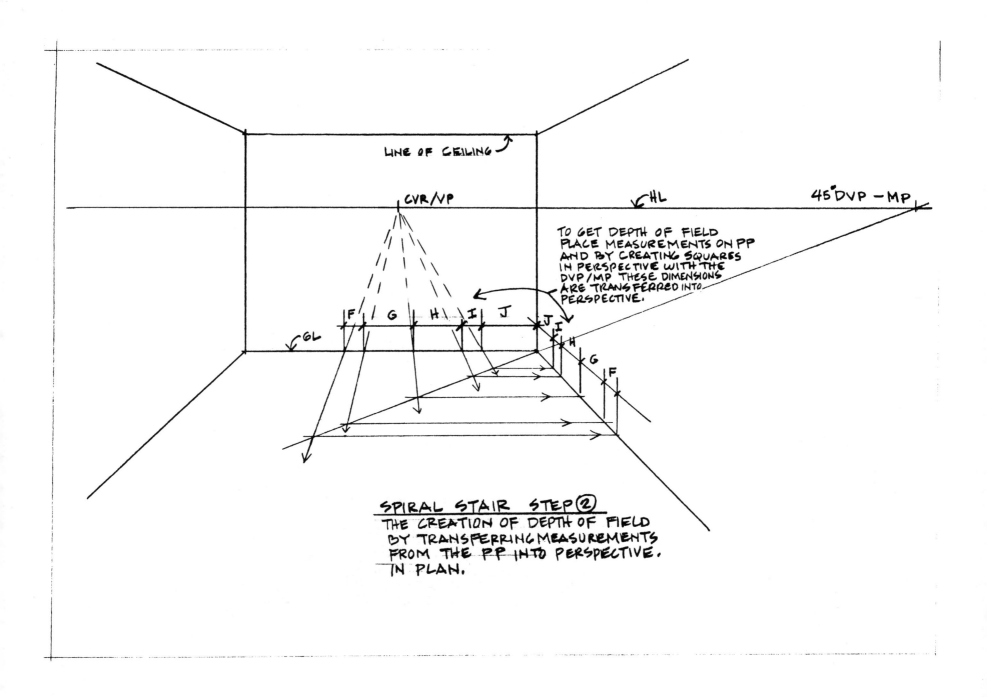

LINE OF CEILING

CVR/VP

HL

45° DVP — MP

TO GET DEPTH OF FIELD
PLACE MEASUREMENTS ON PP
AND BY CREATING SQUARES
IN PERSPECTIVE WITH THE
DVP/MP THESE DIMENSIONS
ARE TRANSFERRED INTO
PERSPECTIVE.

F   G   H   I   J

J
I
H
G
F

GL

SPIRAL STAIR STEP ②
THE CREATION OF DEPTH OF FIELD
BY TRANSFERRING MEASUREMENTS
FROM THE PP INTO PERSPECTIVE.
IN PLAN.

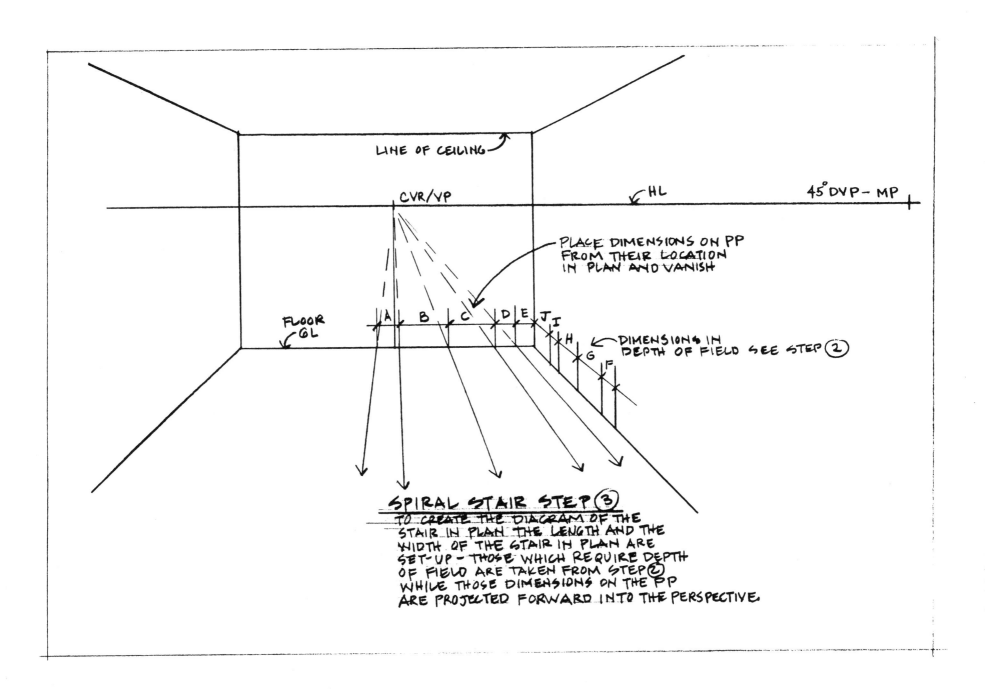

LINE OF CEILING

CVR/VP

HL

45° DVP – MP

PLACE DIMENSIONS ON PP
FROM THEIR LOCATION
IN PLAN AND VANISH

FLOOR
GL

A   B   C   D E J I

H

G

F

DIMENSIONS IN
DEPTH OF FIELD SEE STEP ②

SPIRAL STAIR STEP ③

TO CREATE THE DIAGRAM OF THE
STAIR IN PLAN THE LENGTH AND THE
WIDTH OF THE STAIR IN PLAN ARE
SET-UP – THOSE WHICH REQUIRE DEPTH
OF FIELD ARE TAKEN FROM STEP ②
WHILE THOSE DIMENSIONS ON THE PP
ARE PROJECTED FORWARD INTO THE PERSPECTIVE.

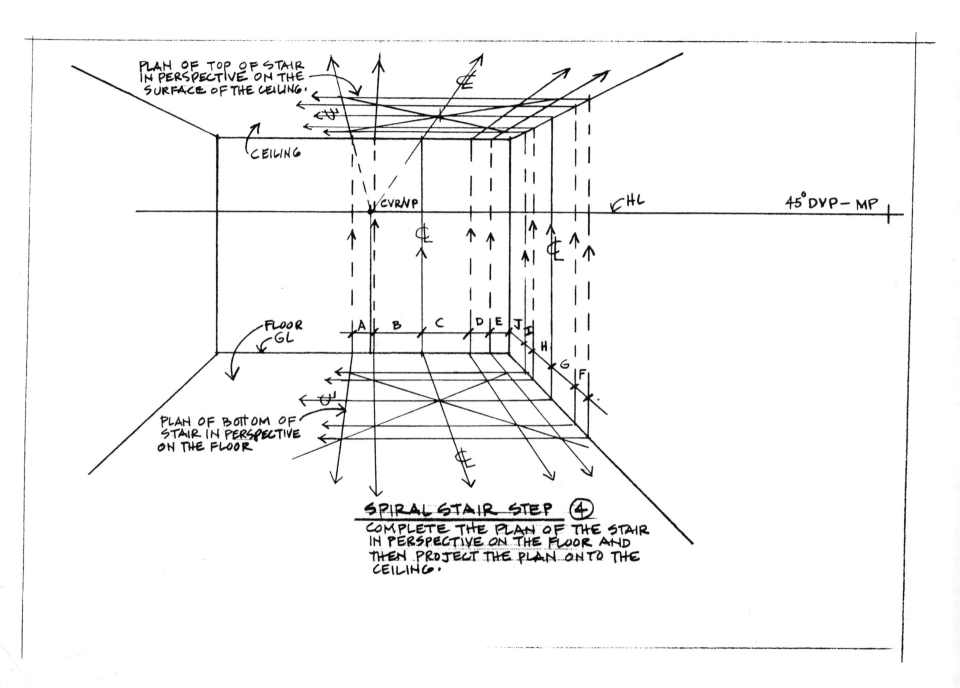

PLAN OF TOP OF STAIR
IN PERSPECTIVE ON THE
SURFACE OF THE CEILING.

CEILING

CVRNP

HL

45° DVP — MP

₵

₵

₵

FLOOR
GL

A   B   C   D E J
                    H
                  G   F

PLAN OF BOTTOM OF
STAIR IN PERSPECTIVE
ON THE FLOOR

₵

SPIRAL STAIR STEP ④
COMPLETE THE PLAN OF THE STAIR
IN PERSPECTIVE ON THE FLOOR AND
THEN PROJECT THE PLAN ONTO THE
CEILING.

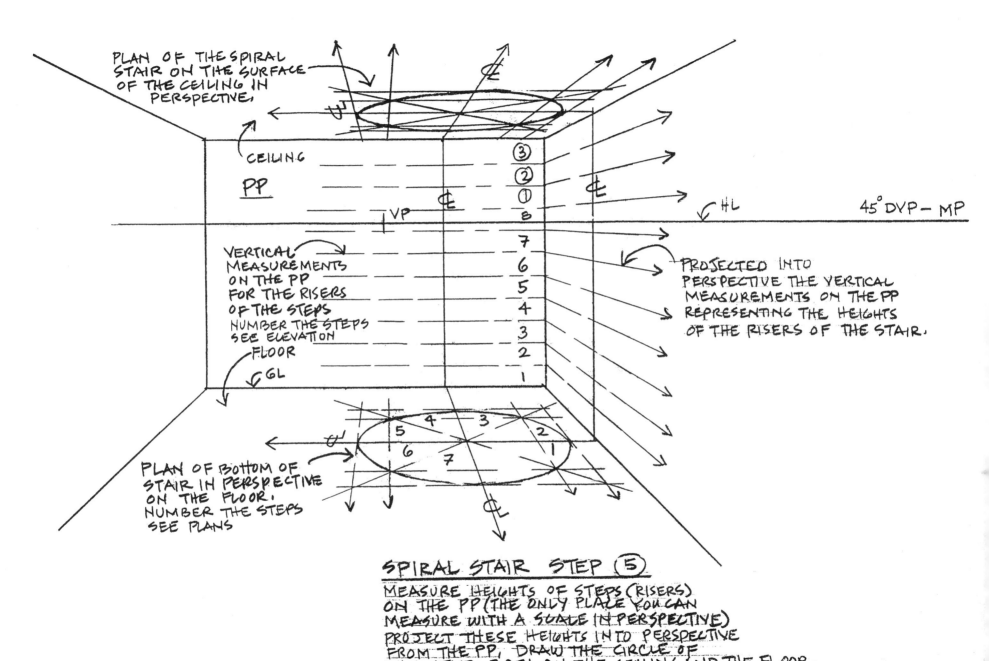

PLAN OF THE SPIRAL
STAIR ON THE SURFACE
OF THE CEILING IN
PERSPECTIVE.

CEILING

PP

Ȼ

VP

VERTICAL
MEASUREMENTS
ON THE PP
FOR THE RISERS
OF THE STEPS
NUMBER THE STEPS
SEE ELEVATION

FLOOR

GL

③
②
①
B
7
6
5
4
3
2
1

HL

45° DVP — MP

PROJECTED INTO
PERSPECTIVE THE VERTICAL
MEASUREMENTS ON THE PP
REPRESENTING THE HEIGHTS
OF THE RISERS OF THE STAIR.

PLAN OF BOTTOM OF
STAIR IN PERSPECTIVE
ON THE FLOOR.
NUMBER THE STEPS
SEE PLANS

5 4 3
6   2
   7 1

SPIRAL STAIR STEP ⑤

MEASURE HEIGHTS OF STEPS (RISERS)
ON THE PP (THE ONLY PLACE YOU CAN
MEASURE WITH A SCALE IN PERSPECTIVE)
PROJECT THESE HEIGHTS INTO PERSPECTIVE
FROM THE PP, DRAW THE CIRCLE OF
THE STAIR BOTH ON THE CEILING AND THE FLOOR.
NUMBER THE STEPS BOTH IN PLAN AND IN
ELEVATION ON THE PP.

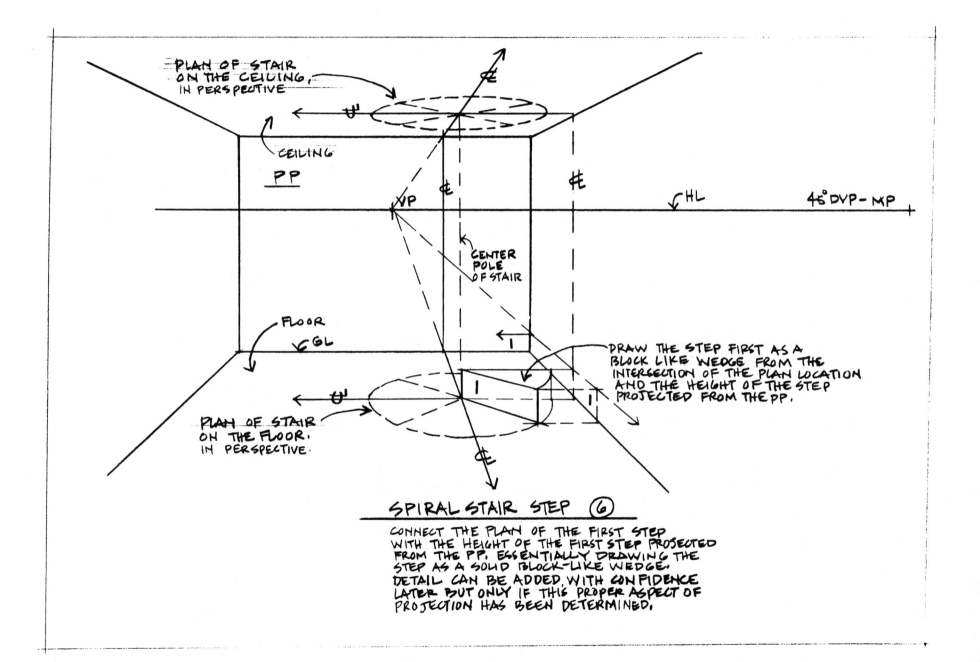

PLAN OF STAIR
ON THE CEILING,
IN PERSPECTIVE

CEILING

PP

CENTER
POLE
OF STAIR

VP

HL

45° DVP-MP

FLOOR

GL

PLAN OF STAIR
ON THE FLOOR,
IN PERSPECTIVE.

DRAW THE STEP FIRST AS A
BLOCK LIKE WEDGE FROM THE
INTERSECTION OF THE PLAN LOCATION
AND THE HEIGHT OF THE STEP
PROJECTED FROM THE PP.

SPIRAL STAIR STEP ⑥

CONNECT THE PLAN OF THE FIRST STEP
WITH THE HEIGHT OF THE FIRST STEP PROJECTED
FROM THE PP. ESSENTIALLY DRAWING THE
STEP AS A SOLID BLOCK-LIKE WEDGE.
DETAIL CAN BE ADDED WITH CONFIDENCE
LATER BUT ONLY IF THIS PROPER ASPECT OF
PROJECTION HAS BEEN DETERMINED.

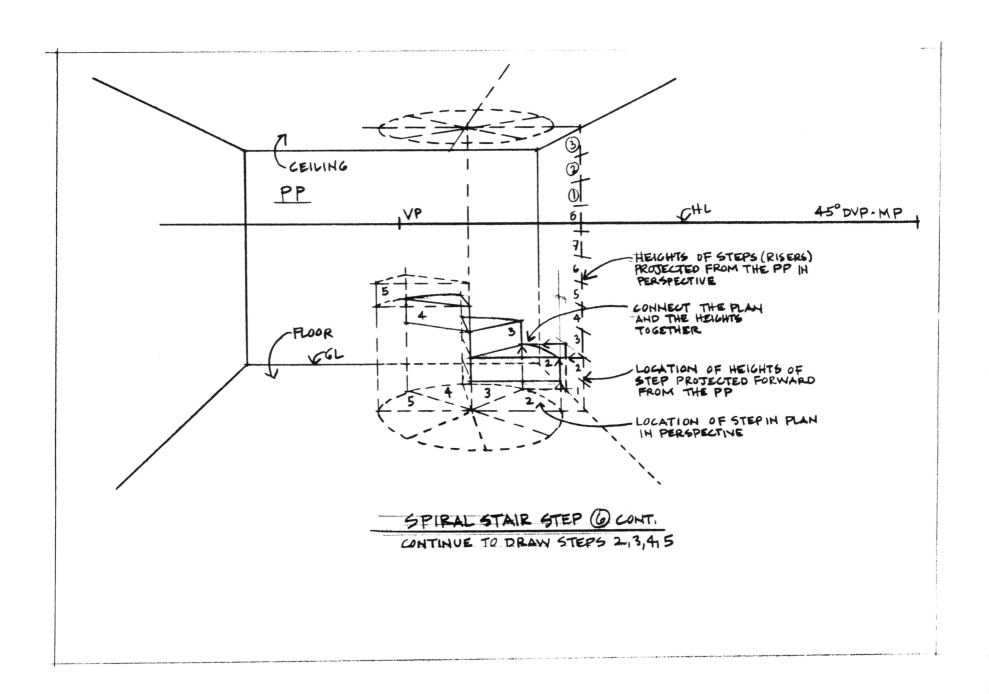

CEILING

PP

VP

⊙HL

45° DVP·MP

③
②
①
8
7
6
5

HEIGHTS OF STEPS (RISERS)
PROJECTED FROM THE PP IN
PERSPECTIVE

5
4
3

CONNECT THE PLAN
AND THE HEIGHTS
TOGETHER

FLOOR

GL

5
4
3
2

2
2

3
4

5

LOCATION OF HEIGHTS OF
STEP PROJECTED FORWARD
FROM THE PP

LOCATION OF STEP IN PLAN
IN PERSPECTIVE

SPIRAL STAIR STEP ⑥ CONT.
CONTINUE TO DRAW STEPS 2, 3, 4, 5

113

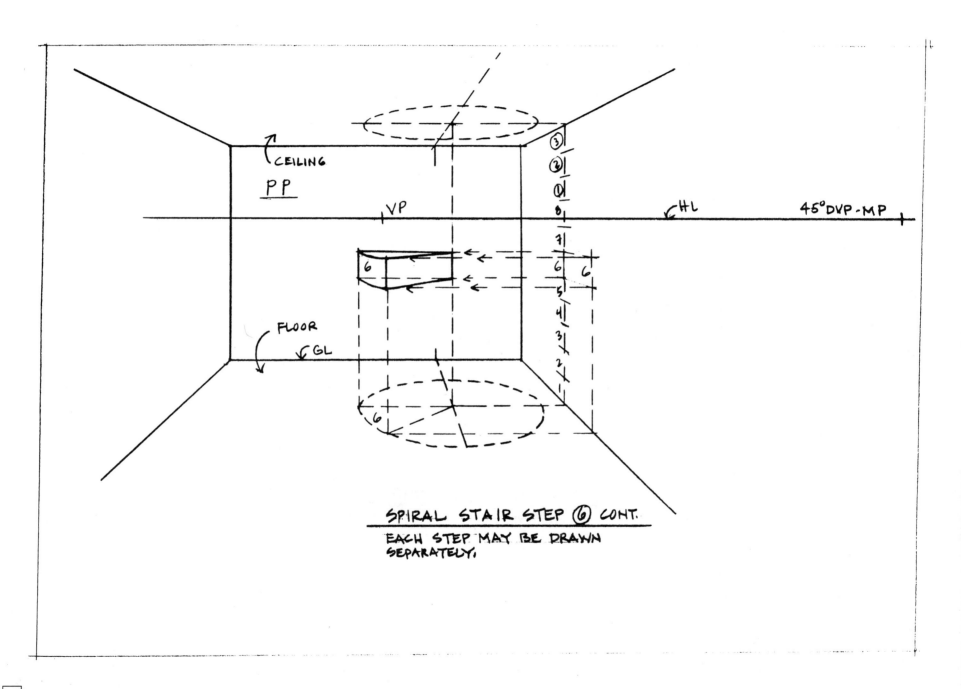

CEILING

PP

VP

HL

45°DVP-MP

③
②
①
0
7
6   6
5
4
3
2
1

6

FLOOR
GL

6

SPIRAL STAIR STEP ⑥ CONT.
EACH STEP MAY BE DRAWN
SEPARATELY.

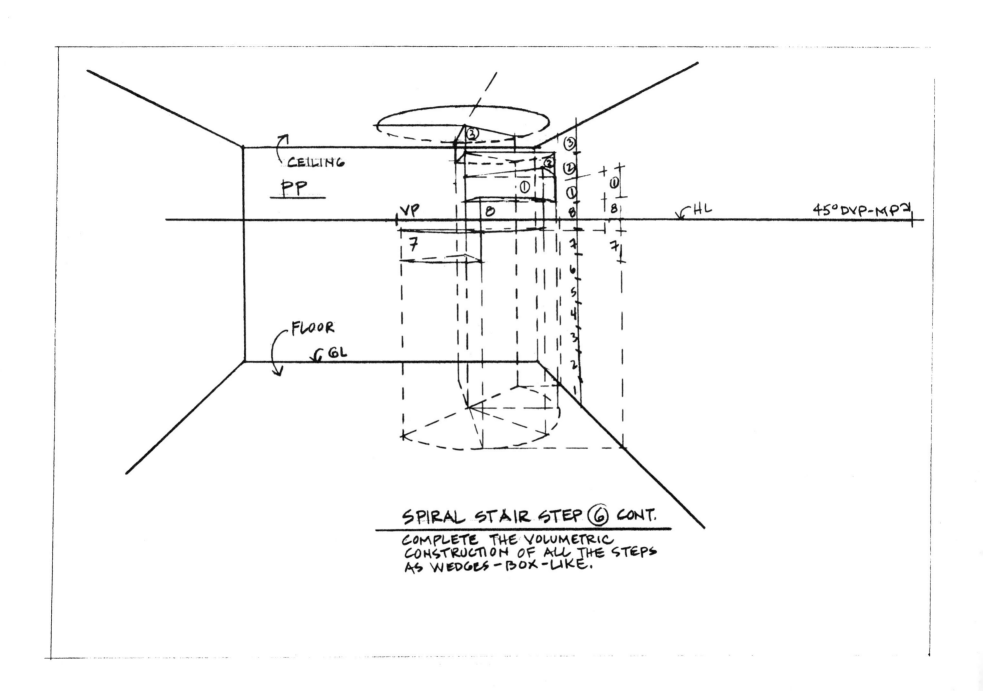

CEILING

PP

VP

FLOOR

GL

HL

45° DVP-MP2

SPIRAL STAIR STEP ⑥ CONT.
COMPLETE THE VOLUMETRIC
CONSTRUCTION OF ALL THE STEPS
AS WEDGES - BOX-LIKE.

16.1

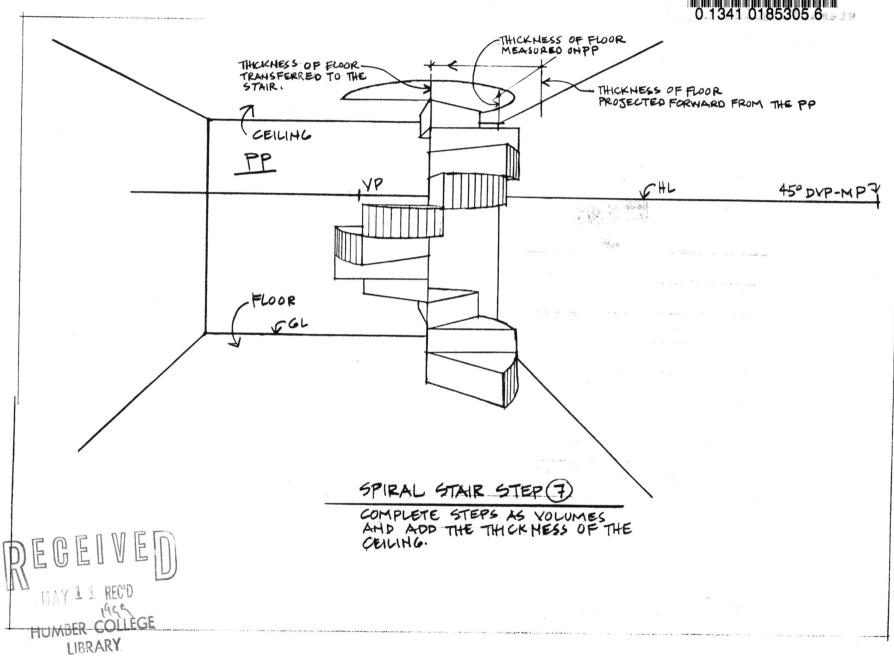

THICKNESS OF FLOOR
MEASURED ON PP

THICKNESS OF FLOOR
TRANSFERRED TO THE
STAIR.

THICKNESS OF FLOOR
PROJECTED FORWARD FROM THE PP

CEILING

PP

VP

HL

45° DVP-MP

FLOOR

GL

SPIRAL STAIR STEP ⑦

COMPLETE STEPS AS VOLUMES
AND ADD THE THICKNESS OF THE
CEILING.